THRESHOLD
EDITIONS

ALSO BY GREG GUTFELD

THE KING OF LATE NIGHT

GREG GUTFELD

THRESHOLD EDITIONS

NEW YORK LONDON TORONTO SYDNEY NEW DELHI

Threshold Editions
An Imprint of Simon & Schuster, Inc.
1230 Avenue of the Americas
New York, NY 10020

First Threshold Editions hardcover edition July 2023

THRESHOLD EDITIONS and colophon are trademarks of Simon & Schuster, Inc.

For information about special discounts for bulk purchases, please contact Simon & Schuster Special Sales at 1-866-506-1949 or business@simonandschuster.com.

The Simon & Schuster Speakers Bureau can bring authors to your live event. For more information, or to book an event, contact the Simon & Schuster Speakers Bureau at 1-866-248-3049 or visit our website at www.simonspeakers.com.

Interior design by Erika R. Genova

Manufactured in the United States of America

10 9 8 7 6 5 4 3 2 1

Names: Gutfeld, Greg, author.
Title: The king of late night / Greg Gutfeld.
Description: New York : Threshold Editions, 2023.
Identifiers: LCCN 2023020146 (print) | LCCN 2023020147 (ebook) | ISBN 9781501190759 (hardcover) | ISBN 9781501190773 (ebook)
Subjects: LCSH: Gutfeld, Greg. | Television personalities—United States—Biography. | Conservatism—United States—Humor. | Political correctness—United States—Humor. | Political satire, American. | BISAC: POLITICAL SCIENCE / Commentary & Opinion | POLITICAL SCIENCE / Political Ideologies / Conservatism & Liberalism | LCGFT: Autobiographies. | Essays.
Classification: LCC PN1992.4.G88 A3 2023 (print) | LCC PN1992.4.G88 (ebook) | DDC 791.4502/8092 [B]—dc23/eng/20230509

LC record available at https://lccn.loc.gov/2023020146
LC ebook record available at https://lccn.loc.gov/2023020147

ISBN 978-1-5011-9075-9
ISBN 978-1-5011-9077-3 (ebook)

To everyone out there who shares the risk today,
and who will share the risk tomorrow

HOW I GOT AWAY WITH FLIPPING THE ENTERTAINMENT WORLD UPSIDE DOWN

We are living in the age of the flip: where everything you assumed to be pretty much stable has been turned on its head, and for the better (mostly). This flip has occurred in nearly every area of life—from art to politics, from cities to humor; from drug policy to your very own perceptions of the universe. This book is, in part, about this phenomenon, but focusing mainly on one precious flip: the reversal of the late-night comedy landscape, performed by yours truly (with immeasurable help from others).

FOREWORD

In the past, the assumption was that the Right was always serious, and rarely funny—as stiff as your dad trying to dance to Earth, Wind & Fire at a wedding, or as unmovable as an abandoned hiker on Mount Everest. In short—as dead as Dan Rather (he's dead, right?).

And of course, it was the Left that took chances and risks with language and ideas—making them perfect comedians. That was true, for a while—when the Left could take a joke way back when. But now, if Richard Pryor or George Carlin were alive, they would run screaming from campuses, chased by a crowd of nonbinary Oberlin students. They would be hanging out with the Babylon Bee before they'd give Colbert or Kimmel the time of day.

We now are the funny people, and everyone else are in a state of anxious denial. Shockingly, this development has been terrible for those other guys at late night.

But awesome for their therapists.

"So (Seth, Jimmy, Stephen, Jimmy) are you still having recurring nightmares about Greg Gutfeld? Any more thoughts of jumping off the chocolate M&M in Times Square when you think about the path you chose for your career? Do you still feel personally responsible for getting Trump elected? Don't answer that, our time is up for today . . . Oh yeah, that'll be $800."

PREFACE ONE

The Letter Informing Me That I Might Be Dying

It's roughly 1984, I'm twenty years old, and I'm coming home from the University of California, Berkeley, to see my mom in sunny San Mateo. For my entire life of living there, we had a mailbox on the left side of the garage door of our small house, where if you felt above the slot, you'd find the cheaply installed button to open the garage. I had my bags over one shoulder, and slipped my fingers in and up, and the door rose up.

I'd done this thousands of times in my life, once I had reached the height in order to do so (at age nineteen). Then when the door stopped at ceiling height, I would peer in to see if there was any mail. We lived in the suburbs, and by "we" I mean me and my mom, a widow. So most of the mail was coupon envelopes, laminated postcards from a local creepy handyman and lawn care specialist (his van never had implements I could plainly recognize as gardening tools), and maybe something that resembled a monthly calendar from the church.

But this time would be different.

There was one thing in that box that I would never forget.

A human finger.

Or more specifically, it was *my* finger, holding a letter from a major hospital, addressed to Mr. Gutfeld. Since I was the only Mr. Gutfeld left in my family, I took all of that mail now. Because, for better or worse, I was now Mr. Gutfeld. I paid some of the bills and answered a lot of the calls. My dad had recently died.

Of what?

Good question.

I killed him. With my bare hands. Oh, sure, he put up a struggle from his hospital bed, but three feet of gauze shoved down anybody's throat will do the trick.

I kid. But since this is only page 2 of the book, why not give you a jolt, to keep you from putting it down. Honestly I've never written about this stuff before, so forgive me for the jokes.

I walked past my mom's Japanese (I can't remember the brand) mini station wagon. Typical of any car driven by a sixty-year-old woman, it was impeccable, not a scratch, with less mileage than what people put on their slippers.

And as always, in the front seat was a large orange cushion from one of the dining chairs that allowed my mom to see beyond the dashboard. Okay, I'm lying. It was for me! But she had hemorrhoids so we both benefited.

On a good day, she might crack four foot eleven. Luckily, God made me a foot taller than her.

My little mother was in the family room, a housecoated, white-haired hellion sitting in a cluttered but somewhat charming paneled front room with an L-shaped couch fit for her and a dog named "Gin," and covered in dog hair—glass ring stains on end tables left from whatever dog-named-infused drink a widow sips. The ironing board was to the right of the oversize heaving box of a TV. Remember the Sony Trinitron? It weighed more than the shut-ins who watched it—as wide as it was deep. Thanks to technology everything gets smaller. Except the people.

Above the couch where my mom would sit to watch whatever one watched in 1983 (I believe it was *Leave It to Beaver*) was a strange painting of a solitary woman, sitting "Indian-style" (Sorry, I meant Elizabeth Warren–style), a gift from my mother's best friend, who had died a decade or so earlier. It was not an attractive painting. I once tried to google the artist to see if we were sitting on a hidden treasure. But from what I gather, no.

It was a painting likely purchased at one of those art sales at roadside motels, when they unload the stuff they used to place above headboards to hide a fist-size hole where the drugs were stashed.

I once examined the painting in detail for any "please help me" S.O.S.'s etched in blood.

We hugged as always and patted each other on our backs—something I do with everyone now—like burping a baby. I pat them and I don't know why, but I do this with everyone. My wife hates it when I do it, but I picked it up from my mom. Never one to analyze my behavior, I assume it's because I never know where to put my hands in a hug—something that was never a problem slow-dancing to the final number at the prom. My mom made an excellent date. Why she had rubbers in her pocketbook is beyond me.

My little mother was built like a hydrant—so much so that if she went to the park in a yellow raincoat, she had to keep moving or dogs would pee on her.

Short, stocky, with a pair of tits that could double as a patio awning, she had a clown's perm of white hair above her wrinkly face and big glasses, framing a face like a congenial French bulldog (her maiden name was Cauhape, which is French for "fuck off"). She'd been through a lot in the last twenty years, and it seemed like, with my father's passing (which I had nothing to do with; I can't stress that enough no matter what that guy on *Dateline* says), the worst was over.

She was always excited to see me, and me to see her—but it was hard to convey that, given that we were both neurotic and easy to set off. A convivial moment could turn dour if she brought up something I didn't want to talk about—and likewise, I could do the same to her. I imagine this is how it is with lots of parents and adult kids. But we were especially combative. I once threw a roll of toilet paper at her, which we both reacted to with shocked hilarity.

It's such a weird thing that the people you know too well, and who know you, too, can't tolerate each other.

It's part of life's equation: It's easy to be charming to people you casually know. But once you get to know someone, you realize that we're all imperfect messes—puzzle pieces that can't fit, even if in our heads we thought we could.

We are all amazingly appealing until we find out how horrible all of us are.

We moved to the kitchen, just off the room past the ironing board, and sat at the swiveled table among the avocado-colored appliances. The kitchen had been redone in the 1970s after my mom's best friend had died. True, when someone kills themselves in your kitchen you gotta redo it, or the food never tastes the same, because of all the sadness—just kidding. She didn't die in the kitchen, but a lot of recipes did.

My mom's pal was a bedridden millionaire, who left my parents three hundred grand or so—which was a lot of money back in the day. I didn't kill her, either.

When she died, my parents, who were low-middle or maybe even middle class, now had appealing choices in their lives. I could go to the all-boys private high school, unlike my older sisters, who were girls and couldn't. Remember, this was the late seventies. Men couldn't get pregnant yet and girls didn't have penises.

They went to public school—Hillsdale High, home to no one famous except the sisters of Greg Gutfeld. Oh and Nick Vanos (RIP).

So they contemplated moving to a bigger house in tonier areas like Hillsborough, homes of people with swimming pools and mistresses who mysteriously drown in them.

We never moved, though—content to stay on a cul-de-sac on Heather Lane (a perfect street name, by the way, for someone who needs a porn name), in a San Mateo hood called Hillsdale, situated between Hillsdale High and Hillsdale Mall. (Hillsdale Mall was the perfect mall of the early 1970's. Outdoor, serene, populated by extras from *Mad Men.).* My sisters went to Hillsdale High. I went to Serra, about one mile away. Unlike me, it was known for sports.

Serra was an all-boy sports powerhouse. I'd already been commuting there, by Schwinn, taking math classes there as an eighth grader before, and it was the first time I really experienced stupidity from above, and not below. Generally as a kid, the dumber kids were younger than you. But in high school, you realized that stupidity was not related to age at all. You could be bullied by a guy who appeared to be in his twenties, but was merely one year older. And God knows whatever was going on in his life that made him want to ruin yours. If anyone had a good life, and was still bullying someone—then that person should die a fiery horrible death. My guess is that person doesn't exist. Also at this age, you discovered adults can be stupid, too.

Like most in that era, our kitchen had an avocado-shaded fridge, a stacked double oven, and the same nauseating green countertops. The kitchen was smaller than most walk-in closets rich New Yorkers have for their vibrators. I think about that kitchen the way you think about the water faucet in grade school. Jesus, we must have been tiny people to operate in these little spaces. But even in that tiny area, it was a dirty mess.

She opened the fridge to show me the sliced selection of deli meats she bought at Petrini's market, as well as the beer. I grabbed two bottles and flipped off their caps, sat down, and pulled the letter out of the stack of crap I had just carried in.

I read it silently to myself, and was not prepared for what it turned out to be.

But it all made some final sense when I look back at the final years of my dad's life.

It might not even be true. But I'm not a doctor, and certainly not a reliable narrator given I am writing this affected by the grape.

I read it aloud, and now, forgive me, but it's not verbatim. But I'll do my best to re-create it.

> *Dear Mr. Gutfeld, we are informing you that during your past surgery, the blood used in the transfusion had been drawn from a blood supply contaminated with HIV. We need you to come in and be tested for HIV at your earliest blah blah blah.*

I didn't add that "blah blah blah." It was in the letter . . . just like that!

I kid, I don't remember the rest, and you might not remember much about this era—but this sort of HIV contamination was a big problem back then. As AIDS raged across the country, bureaucrats were slow to stop the spread because they didn't want to seem like they were targeting a specific group of people (the black Irish, obviously). To deal with the spread from blood banks, they would have to ban gays from giving blood. Good luck with that.

They eventually did, but not after some people got infected (I believe tennis great Arthur Ashe was one of them).

I know this sort of thing sounds terrible, doesn't it! Awful.

To get a letter that says my dad may have AIDS. Especially since he couldn't have AIDS, as he was already dead.

It's definitely not a joking matter. Not something to use for some afternoon prankery. Except for me and my mom, it was.

The letter wasn't really for me, but for my dad. And he was dead. Maybe from AIDS, but perhaps also from other shit. Who really knows. I didn't and I don't ever claim to know for sure. But it made sense, the way he had declined so quickly in a year, after holding on for so long. (He had Cancer for fifteen years. Cancer was the name of our beagle. Just kidding again; I'll stop.)

My mom had first told me he was sick when I was eight years old, in second grade. Now, up to then, I had had a good run. Had already learned to read. Was pretty good on the math time tables. Was cultivating spontaneous boners when time would allow. So this, in my opinion, was that *first* moment when life interrupted childhood.

Remember, childhood has almost no real nod to mortality. Your magical grandmother might have passed on—but she was such a strange mystical being you assumed she floated away on a laser beam. You have to remember this: that we all assume that everyone we knew looked "that" way all their lives. Your grandma was always a grandma. Your mom always a mom, at that age. So death was not an aging process, to our young minds. It was removal of sorts—in which a beloved was taken somewhere else.

I wonder how that changes now, when you have social media, mass shootings, and everything—including birth, aging, and death—is recorded. Do children understand mortality far earlier? I can't begin to understand how that works. Humans, as is, are the only living creatures that know they will die. It's likely cruel to introduce that reality even sooner than it needs to be. I think about my dog. If he has no concept of death, then what is his problem? Hunger? Pain? Isolation has to be weird when death isn't on your list of fears.

In that same kitchen, she told me that "daddy isn't well." While she was peeling potatoes or something, over the sink—I remember her crying. It shows up in dreams. That scene. A lot happened in that kitchen. My mom was a terrible cook.

I was eighteen before I realized macaroni and cheese shouldn't twitch.

As her vision got worse, so did her cooking. She'd be like, "Why doesn't this turkey fit in the oven?" I'd be like, "Mom, that's the bread box!"

She'd keep things well past their sell date. If something looked old, or curled up, or greenish—you'd just lop it off like it was a gangrene finger. We didn't need everything to be 100 percent edible. We didn't make the "perfect the enemy of the good," especially when it came to a moss-covered liverwurst.

We would find things in our food that might be considered choking hazards, although that could describe most of her dishes.

Things like a Band-Aid, clip-on earrings, or car keys. It got so bad I'd wave a metal detector over the meat loaf before I cut it.

That kitchen, by the way, was where I went through the worst drug trip of my life, while my parents made fun of me. The avocado theme didn't help. But I smoked weed that may have been laced with angel dust (a common rumor at the time to scare people from getting high), and I ended up in the ER. The pot came from one of my sister's boyfriends, a tennis instructor and low-level pot dealer. My guess is, it was just strong weed. But I learned to never smoke pot again, or play tennis. The last time I saw the tennis bro, he had handed me a large box of porn mags through my bedroom window since he was leaving town. He might have been he most corrupting influence in my life. Or Santa Claus.

As a kid, I didn't understand my mom's bad news about my dad at first, but later it started to make devastating sense. Turns out he had cancer first diagnosed when I was four years old. Thyroid cancer. They removed it, put him on meds, and he ended up doing fine. They would give him an expiration date (usually it was three to four years—stuff you'd only hear in soap operas—"Vic, you have two years, tops"), and he'd always surpass it. Until I was nineteen. He started really declining, fast. (My dad's cancer, apparently, can be traced to the hundreds of X-rays he got as a child when he broke his back. Unlike me, he was an athlete and continued to run track in a back brace. My theory is, he was running only against other white guys so it was easy. At least that's what I tell myself, as a non-fast runner.)

A lot of people can remember when they first were told about the "birds and the bees."

I do. I had asked my mom where I came from—maybe I was six at the time. She gave me shockingly specific details. "You came from a hole between my legs."

That was it. One thing about my mom, no matter what the subject, she never was one to beat around the bush.

But I also wonder, when did we find out about our own mortality? When does the concept of death—our death, not others'—come into view?

I believe it happened for me in that kitchen the day I got that AIDS letter. The thought that we were all gonna die, some sooner than others. The letter was addressed to me, not just to my dad.

Fact is—the letter made total sense, given everything I'd seen before. When I was home from high school, along with my mother, I would take care of cleaning my father's bedsores and assorted wounds, which I figured derived from him being bedridden from cancers that riddled his body for years. I would "exercise" his legs by pushing them toward his chest until he would scream, and do other moves prescribed by a therapist.

I would remove the dressing, wash the wounds, and repeat. Believe me, I was no Florence Nightingale. Although if you saw me throw a football you might argue with that opinion.

It was my mother who did this round the clock—and I or my sisters would pick up the slack when she couldn't deal with it. But in the last few years of my dad's life, his condition had gotten dramatically worse. The weight loss accelerated, as well as these sores.

Side note: When my dad was bedridden, he hated my music so much he would climb out of the bed in total pain into a wheelchair and struggle across the living room to my bedroom to poke and prod the bedroom door with a crutch to plead with me to turn it down. At that time it was Sex Pistols, Dead Kennedys, Ramones, and Clash nonstop. And at a ridiculous volume. I remember him saying, "Greg, please stop—this is Nazi music!" Which wasn't true. I had stopped listening to ABBA years ago. (I also remember, on a very important night of my life—prom—my dad fell out of his wheelchair and I yelled at him, in my cheap tux, for making me late for my date. My best friend, Mike Geitz, looked at me in horror, saying, "That's your dad." I cannot forget that moment.)

So anyway, this letter had either explained what my mother and I had seen up close, or it meant nothing—other than bad timing and the worst record keeping ever. My advice to hospitals: Don't send letters to your dead patients. They seldom get read and it's a waste of trees.

I'm pretty sure Dad was taken to that hospital after he croaked.

I read the letter to my mom, and she chuckled. We both knew what we were going to do.

Because like any adolescent growing up before star-69, I loved crank calls.

"Hello, [Redacted, or whatever] Hospital, can I help you?"

(That was the actual name of the hospital. "Redacted Hospital.")

"Yes, I'm Mr. Gutfeld, and I'm responding to a letter you sent me."

I gave my dad's name, and they went to look up my information. I have no idea what they did at this point, because, I mean, did they have computers in 1983 or '84?

"Just a moment, sir."

They returned and asked me how I was doing, and I said, "Great, just a slight cough."

The person disappeared and ended up coming back and saying that yes, I would need to come in and get tested for HIV, because of a contaminated blood transfusion during the removal of a tumor on my shoulder.

I responded with surprise. "Oh wow, that is not good news. So you need to have me come into the hospital?"

"As soon as it is convenient," she said.

"Okay, well, I'd love to get there as soon as possible, but there is a problem."

Here I paused for dramatic effect.

"I've been dead for a year!"

"You have?"

"Yes, can't you hear it in my voice?

"Yes, it's true. I'm dead. So I just wanted to call and let you know that yes, I am dead. In fact I believe my body was delivered to your hospital. You might have handled the cremation!"

Funny side story: I drove to Half Moon Bay to throw the ashes into the ocean, and due to the high winds, all of my dad's ashes ended up all over me and in my mouth. Also, they really aren't "ashes" at all. More like paint chips, soot, and gravel. I told this humorous story on dates to gain sympathy to amplify my odds for sexual congress.

There was more silence from the other end—but then my mom and I broke out laughing and I hung up. We laughed uncontrollably, like two thirteen-year-old boys.

I never followed up on that conversation.

Did I mention I had the coolest hard-drinking old lady in the world for a mom? If I haven't, I probably didn't need to: it's obvious.

PREFACE 2

A Quiz

It's a short one.

Very simple.

What are things you can laugh at?

A. You can laugh at everything.

B. You can't laugh at certain things.

C. Eggs.

What are the things you can't laugh at?

A. You can laugh at everything.

B. You can't laugh at certain things.

C. Eggs.

There is a logic to this. It's the difference between being human and being psychotic.

And the equation is opposite what you think.

It goes like this:

If you know something is really bad (a bunch of people died in a sinking ship, etc.), and in your head you come up with a joke, you're okay. You're fine.

But if you make the joke because that tragedy is not really tragic to you . . . then you're psychotic.

Not knowing that something is bad, and making a joke about it, doesn't excuse you from making the joke. It means you're nuts. Completely.

But if you know something *is* truly awful (9/11, a mass shooting, Jesse Watters's hair plugs, Joy Behar's voice, Brian Kilmeade's taste in neckties, pediatric cancer) and you have not only an urge to make a joke, but actually one to tell—you're not just super healthy, you're *someone I definitely want to be around.*

You see how this seems like a reversal of common decency. If someone makes a joke because they're unaware of the subject matter's horribleness, they should be excused. And the person who makes the joke knowing it's a terrible tragedy is the bad guy. I don't think so. *It's the opposite.*

Joking about tragedy is not being sick. It's being healthy. It's how we cope with life, which is horrifying, each and every day of our existence. Think of it as a natural immunity against depression. Especially if you're my neighbor. It's the thesis of Kat Timpf's first book, which I loom over like an inspirational godlike shadow.

Here's a confession: during the last segment on *The Five* called "One More Thing," I tend to think of the very worst things you could possibly think—whenever the "one more thing" by a fellow panelist turns out to be somber or sad or an even uplifting subject.

I know that it's totally wrong to say it, but it's screaming in my head, only because the sheer horribleness of my thoughts are my only way of dealing with it.

If a cohost talks about the death of an elderly icon, or a child going through some rough medical procedure, my head races with the worst things one could say about such topics. I'm talking about the very worst things that you can think of—but perhaps even worse, because this is my best and most exercised muscle. If I only used my pecs this much, I'd be on a spray bottle of Mr. Clean.

And you'll never know what thoughts I'm thinking because I don't say them.

If you consider that bad, you can go screw yourself. Because there's a difference between thinking something and saying something. If you don't agree, then you're essentially advocating for thought-crime punishment, and you're no longer invited to my funeral. Or my hot tub, which, by the way, will be present at my funeral. I'm gonna have the hearse pulling one with my closest friends in it. I think I got the idea from watching *Pimp My Ride* on MTV with a very wasted Bret Baier.

There is absolutely nothing better in life than being with someone, and upon hearing somber news, looking into each other's eyes . . . and knowing that both are thinking of something truly awful. There are times with Kat Timpf and Tyrus where we will look at each other and know that we are contaminating this moment using the same shared, perverse, snake-ridden, rat-filled brain. We will stare deep into our eyes, until that moment passes and nod to each other. We never speak of what we think, but we share it. It's the closest example of psychic communication on the planet. Except for the connection I have with the Central Park squirrels. (No matter what they tell me, I will not assassinate the park's arborist.)

There are times when you might know, on *The Five*, that I am thinking a terrible thought.

Usually when I'm looking at Geraldo Rivera's mustache. My dead giveaway is when I express a trite platitude that you know I would normally despise.

The platitude that I hate the most is "You go, girl," which is expressed whenever some teenage girl shoots a basket with only one arm, from a wheelchair with her therapy chicken nearby.

How can that great achievement be wrong? It isn't wrong at all—which makes me want to think of the very thing that violates that moment. I don't like safe topics even if they're truly wholesome.

So I always add "You go, girl," but in my head I'm visualizing

LeBron James swatting the ball away right off the top of the poor girl's head.

Thinking bad thoughts is your right. It's also a right to say them, too, although you might want to wait until you're in good company or at least have a running start on bad company—or be filthy, fuck-you rich. It's easy to think good thoughts, and it's easy to think bad thoughts. But it's good to think bad thoughts when you're supposed to think good ones. Why? To test the boundaries, I guess.

A recurring concept in this book is the reversal of stereotypical stances and assumptions. The Right going to the left, the Left turning right. It's one flip we've watched in real time: the Left, once the haven for free speech, is now a bounty hunter for the truly outspoken—tracking the violators, and destroying careers. Meaning it's people like myself or Tyrus or Kat who are the new defenders. The Left is now the old fart pushing censorship, and the Right is the side championing the offensive. We're like the General Pattons of objectionable. The Schwarzkopf of inappropriate! You get the idea. If you don't, I'll promise to do better in the next chapter.

The Comedy Flip

I've never had a job in my life where I get to tell strangers what I do for a living. But now I get to do this here, in this book.

It's not a problem for me. I enjoy it. You guys know what I do and I know why you like it, and we don't need to exchange pleasantries—we can just chat like old friends.

But I never get to talk about how this whole thing happened. I can tell you why it happened. But not how. So why not do that here!

That's what this book is really about: the flip of an entire scene—one you might define as late-night comedy—and how it was fueled in part by me.

This late night show, *Gutfeld!*, has now turned the late night category on its head, and obviously it was an uphill battle—one I've fought for twenty years. It's one of the flips among many that you see happening: suburban life is now cooler than cities; progressive feminists now protect men more so than women; criminals are now considered victims, while their victims are now their oppressors by way of their ancestry.

In comedy, since God knows when, we lived in an entertainment aquarium where the Left owned the space, and it was one that they wouldn't share with others. They created their own little universe and you weren't invited—which allowed them to pretend that they were the champions of risk. Except that for the most part they were as edgy as a soggy Nerf Ball. Left-wing comedians literally all looked alike. Except that Patton Oswalt looked like Andy Richter's morning stool.

They saw themselves as daring, yet they couldn't be in the same room with people who didn't share their opinions. How is it daring when all the people who would be in charge of censoring you (the networks) agree with you? How is it daring when the media simply nods along to your shared worldview?

I realized this early on, and I decided to take the turf from them.

It took some time—years, in fact—but I did it.

Or rather we did.

And it went exactly as planned.

I am lying.

First—the Name and the Exclamation Point

So let's work backward . . .

People ask me how *Gutfeld!* got its name.

Well, first of all, *Maude* was already taken. And they wouldn't allow my second choice, which was *FU Mr. Peterson*. (Mr. Peterson was a guidance counselor who offered no guidance or counsel.)

But it does have a decent backstory, if you wanna hear it. And if you bought this book, it doesn't matter if you don't. I already have your money.

Right now as I write this, *Gutfeld!* is the number one show in late night, and it did so coming out of nowhere.

As Walter Kirn describes it, it's like a sandlot player entering the major leagues and pitching a string of no-hitters against the old pros. Sure, my string of no-hitters is coming against guys who couldn't make the Toledo Mud Hens, but a no-hitter is a no-hitter! (Which I think is a jai-alai reference.)

I love telling this story because it has a happy ending—one that keeps becoming happier every day. (I hope I don't end up eating those words as I finally get nabbed for unsolved murders that I had tried to pin on Brian Kilmeade by dousing the victims with Aqua Velva.)

I remember when I offered my show name to the bosses.

I sent a sheet that simply said "GUTFELD!"

The response?

Silence.

Now, silence is not the opposite of communication.

It's just a different kind of communication.

And it always is telling you something.

Yes, it sounds like a cliché—but anyone who's been married knows that.

The only thing worse than being yelled at is not being yelled at at all.

It means you really blew it. There might be no going back.

I'd honestly just prefer to be hit over the head with a lamp, provided it's not a lava lamp that pours melting molten rock all over my beautiful features. That's what happened to Madonna.

Whether you're in a fight with the wife, or in court, or in a jail cell or an office with human resources, talking is a sign that things can be resolved. Silence means it's bad news all around.

In this case, the silence was telling me: "Greg, what the hell is with the exclamation point?"

Honestly, I didn't think much of it—I had simply shortened the original title that I really wanted for the show. For a long time, I would fantasize that the title for this show that didn't exist would be "THE WORLD SCREAMS GUTFELD!"

Because that's how I felt about the show, or the need for it.

The world was screaming for it!!

"THE WORLD SCREAMS GUTFELD!"

Isn't that great?

I still look at it and think it's a better title than just *Gutfeld!*

But then again, it has my name in it.

It wouldn't work if it was "THE WORLD SCREAMS DOOCY!"

But it reflected my feeling about the fear and trepidation that had turned comedy into a landscape of meek cowardice.

Every time you looked for something that stank of danger in the world of late night comedy, you would come up empty. There was a giant hole there—and I'm *great* at filling big holes.

Before, you had David Letterman, who was not just amazingly good, but also tremendously weird. But his weirdness came from his choices of staffers and guests. He had Chris Elliott, the very best lunatic on television. For my money, Elliott is and was the most engaging person on TV. When he was on, I couldn't take my eyes off him, the same way I was with Liberace when I was ten.

Since then, there was nothing like that. Till now. This show is a direct descendant of Elliott's comedy.

I could see this gap beckoning me in late-night

entertainment—a giant black hole that invited me to dive right in—to plunder, hunker down, relax, stretch out, take a dump, and then take over.

I have no beef with the Jimmys (Kimmel, Fallon), and I could barely care about *The Daily Show* and Stephen Colbert and all the other stuff. To me they were just the restaurants in Times Square that fed the tourists. It's the safe stuff that keeps people fat and full, and the providers gainfully employed.

You could get that anywhere, but I figure there were smart kids out there who would want to find something better. I knew I could be that <u>dive bar</u> everyone hears about, but can't find at first—but once they find it, it's the place they'd never want to leave. It's the joint they'd want to join.

That's how I operated in every job I had. *Men's Health. Stuff. Maxim. Huffington Post. Red Eye. Gutfeld!* Panera Bread.

Make something unique that doesn't exist and then simply see what happens. (It's why I rarely cook.)

Usually good things do! And if they don't—I'll get fired in no time. Which has happened on a few occasions.

So again, I was going to create that thing—but it was gonna be weirder and more surprising and way better than anything before it.

In a world of cheesy Times Square restaurants, this was going to be the raucous dive bar filled with wild games and cheap drinks. It would gleefully offer to the consumer what they could not find anywhere else: entertainment that was lean and not loaded with fat and filler.

I actually drew the title of the show out more than a dozen times using my favorite writing instrument—the Sharpie.

Not enough has been said about the Sharpie.

I love Sharpies—they are the jolly fat people of writing utensils—a thick, wonderful expression of life that runs out of gas in a few hours. Once they dry up, I donate them to the homeless (I throw them out a car window).

My suggestion is, if you want to create something fun, always use Sharpies to sketch it out. That thick swath of black or red or blue triggers a sense of confidence that may not have existed in your brain before you wrote it down. But try to use it on paper, not interns. HR has gotten so unreasonable!

I really do believe that when I gave up the ballpoint pen for the Sharpie, my life changed. In fact, you can tell just by looking at the mess of papers that sit in front of me on *The Five*. You can actually see the madman scribbles—mainly because I write large enough so anyone can see my notes from the recliner at home. Or the International Space Station.

I do this so I can not-so-secretly pull a side glance downward to grab a thought that might have escaped me when my mind goes blank. Fact is, my eyesight is terrible. So bad that I have conversations with short blondes I believe to be Dana

Perino but who actually are complete strangers. I once asked Justin Bieber what it was like working for George W. Bush.

But I'm not always the culprit.

One afternoon, Dana and I were walking up Sixth Avenue. A woman ran up to Dana to tell her she was her biggest fan! She added, "I love you!" Then she said, "You're my favorite weather girl," referring of course to Janice Dean, the weather machine. That's the day I found out Dana will use her pepper spray on anyone for anything. She blasted the woman in the face with it, and then I think she said something to the effect of "I got your five-day forecast right here, bitch!"

Dana proceeded to get her in a headlock chokehold until the woman tapped out. God, she's a little toughie.

But back to me. I would often write my name in big fat juicy letters and above my name scribble, "The World Screams . . ."

I admit it sounds egomaniacal. Which is one reason why I loved it so.

But it had a mission statement built into it. It wasn't like other shows that were either just the person's name or the name plus some weird additional word. Like *Factor* or *Angle*.

What's a factor or an angle?

The Gutfeld Factor sounds like a salve for your colon.

I wonder how many great books have been ruined by terrible titles. Like the Bible.

No offense, but I would have called it "You're Not Gonna Believe This!" by Jesus H. Christ.

Could a name ruin a show?

Fox did a show called *The Specialists*. But after three weeks, they ran out of specialists.

Gutfeld! was definitely better than that, you'd never run out of me. But still, it muted feedback.

Was it anxiety over the exclamation point? Apparently nobody puts exclamation points in show titles—something I never really noticed before.

But no one wanted to bring it up. Except for my favorite host with a hairpiece, Jesse Watters.

He came up to me one day and said, "Hey, congrats on the exclamation point." I thought he really meant it. Then he happily delivered this kill shot: "It really worked for Jeb!"

I hadn't thought of that. Jeb Bush. Jeb frickin' Bush.

He walked off to reattach his "hair system," which had been loosened by some local birds who mistook it for a dead rodent. It's amazing that it holds together, but it explains why he rarely does segments outside anymore. And who knew transparent chinstraps were a thing?

Apparently everyone, except for Jesse, was too scared to tell me the show name was a bad idea.

I suppose the reason for it being a bad idea was that it seems hokey. Do you really believe you need an exclamation point to announce your arrival, like you're something special? No, I didn't. It meant something else entirely.

But part of my charm is you never know the intentions of my decisions.

What did I intend with the exclamation point?

Well, I'll tell you.

The *Red Eye* Influence: The First Step at Flipping Pop Culture at 3 a.m. When No One Was Watching [Thankfully]

The reason for the exclamation point comes from my nightly show *Red Eye*, the deviant mess of a show that's now considered a cult legend by people who missed its charm the first time around. And that was a lot of people. The show aired at 3 a.m., which had its positives and negatives. (It originally aired at 2 a.m., but it was considered too raw for even that hour. "It airs at 9 p.m. in Hawaii" was their concern.) The negative was that most viewers were insomniacs, meth heads, and lonely prop comics. The positive: Notice how I didn't include Fox execs? We were able to screw up, experiment, and be complete idiots—cuz our bosses were asleep.

Back in the *Red Eye* days, when I would get ready for the show, and get hooked up with microphones and earpieces, my sound guy Tony White would get into my ear from the control room and shout "Gutfeld!" He wouldn't say, "Hey, Greg, it's Tony—just checking in to see if you can hear me." Instead, Tony would yell "GUTFELD!" like he'd caught me stealing his lunch from the fridge or something (which I would do at times to keep him healthy).

This was one of the most important things anyone ever did for me, as far as TV goes.

It would not just wake me up—it would get me in the right frame of mind, reminding me that I was doing something exciting and different. It was an opportunity, a gift, a magical moment to do something new every day. You need that. I <u>need</u> that.

He reminded me that it wasn't a chore, it was a gift—to actively engage strangers in a totally legal fashion, for once. I owed him so much for this, I stopped stealing his belongings from his work locker.

This is super important. In all of life. If you aren't careful you can forget the things that make life fun—because over time you took them for granted. That's what repetition does. It does that for everything except eating chicken and masturbation, two things nobody on the planet, at least that I know, is sick of (just don't mix the two, no matter what they show you on TikTok).

Suddenly the things that are novel, exciting, and fraught with joy and risk become as mundane as brushing your teeth, something I try to do weekly.

That's a real problem with me—I get bored fast. Ask my four ex-wives and the three dogs, and the two cats I dropped off in the woods upstate in the middle of the night.

When I get bored, I get in trouble.

When I am bored, I start coming up with bizarre ideas—and then I end up confusing the hell out of my coworkers. Then I get depressed. Suddenly my mood will change, and I will look at my job as a pain in the ass—something to get through, instead of something to enjoy. Boredom turns me into a terrible creature.

I could really make myself and others miserable if I forgot that what I was doing was pretty damn awesome.

When I start to think that what I'm doing is mundane, I do what I can to undermine it. I've been doing this all my life. And it can end badly. It's like that guy Julius Caesar hired to follow him around and say to him, "Caesar is mortal, Caesar is mortal." I need a little voice telling me, "Don't destroy it. Don't destroy it." It's why I hired Tyrus.

At the start of *Red Eye*, I was talented but incompetent, at least in the machinations of television. I knew nothing about how it all worked. I had a close-knit group that worked with me, but when things would fall apart, or I would make a mistake reading the teleprompter, it became easy to blame someone else for everything—and that's what would happen. (Holy shit, I just realized how much I have in common with our current president!

Sometimes I would blame people for things they had nothing to do with, simply because I didn't know what other people did to make the show work.

I would scream at the cameraman for a problem with sound, and then blame the sound guy for some mistake I made while reading a tease. Of course, I found out later . . . it was Shannon Bream, sabotaging me all along.

Actually, it was the result of my own ignorance. When you throw someone in a pool who can't swim, he immediately blames the lifeguard. That was me.

But then I figured it out. Once I realized that I could turn my incompetence into a charming part of the show, it all suddenly fit. Doing things wrong, and admitting that you do them wrong, opened a whole world to connect to the viewer. My fuckups became one of my own weapons. The success of the current late show now rests upon the fact that I make fun of myself more than I do my so-called targets.

The Flip: From Terrified to the Terrifier

I am writing this sentence in a hotel room in Los Angeles. I took a week off from work to get away from distractions and definitely not creditors, and left the show in the capable hands of my talented, amazing crew.

The first show was to be hosted by someone who hadn't worked the teleprompter in months. The person stumbled during rehearsal and texted me a string of panicky missives ranging from "My god I suck" to "I should quit my job!" and then said "I just can't do this." (If only Kamala Harris or Joe Biden had such a sense of self-awareness.) And, finally, "Where's that twenty you owe me?" I wrote back telling the host how silly this was. It didn't help at all. I didn't know why.

But then it struck me that the person was me. I had done the same fucking thing, over and over again.

I also thought the teleprompter was my enemy once. I remembered then, I was about the same age—midthirties—when I was this fearful. . . .

I was standing in front of Emmaus Bakery early one morning smoking a cigarette. Emmaus is a small country town nestled outside Allentown, PA.

It was the first day of a new job. I never smoked in the morning—hell, I rarely smoked at all. But there I was on a cold winter morning, on Main Street, puffing away, waiting for my best friend Mark Golin to meet up with me before I went to work. Mark had worked with me at *Prevention* magazine, as well as start-up mags like *Exec* and a muscle mag I can't remember the name of. When he showed up, he wore a look of curious exasperation.

"What's your problem?" he asked me.

I told him, "I can't do this. I just can't do this. I'm not ready."

He looked at me, and said, "You're going from fitness editor of *Prevention* magazine to senior writer at *Men's Health*. You aren't fucking joining the goddamn space program. The only person who thinks this is hard is you. No one else does. Jesus Christ. I can't believe this is why you called me out here."

That's what you call a valuable *reframing*.

Every now and then you need it. I can now look back and notice that the fear was due to leaving something familiar for the unknown—and it's something we all worry about.

What drives the worry is that you're leaving an area where you're confident and heading to an area where you might be exposed as an imposter. But it's the only path you can take, and the reframing that works is to replace fear with curiosity. And that becomes something called "learning."

But the one central fact that undermines that fear—is what everyone at work secretly knows: no one really knows what they're doing—until they do it over and over again.

Until then, no one knows if they're the best, or the worst. If you think that you're obviously incompetent, you fail to realize that everyone on your staff—given any moment of the day—feels that way.

Once you realize that, you CAN DO ANYTHING.

Well, okay, not "anything." I'm pretty sure I still can't dunk a basketball without a medium-size stepladder.

But that was a big flip. I changed.

The world's biggest example: Donald Trump. Love him or hate him, he became president, and it didn't bother him the slightest that he'd never been president before. To him, it was an adventure. In his head, he knew that everyone who had done it before had been terrified of doing it. Or, rather, terrified of doing just about anything. I am now convinced that I can be president.

But the first step was for me to host *Red Eye*.

The Foreign Policy Flip

When the initial reports of Russia building forces along the Ukraine border came in, I could feel the galvanizing force of these stories speeding up and accumulating to create a narrative that only goes in one direction.

I understood why: it's the invaded who experienced the atrocity first.

But within months, as the war reporting became background noise, the billions flowed from American taxpayers to somewhere, someplace, in Ukraine.

It was interesting to see the Left, however, smacking their drum to the beat of war.

It was the Right trying to say "Hold on a minute." Sure, you had the neocons, doing the neocon thing. But a strong vibe of anti-warism vibrated from the Right.

It's a flip that makes you wonder—would the Left have been so supportive if Trump had been pushing for billions in military aid to fight Russia? I doubt it. If Trump had wanted to aid Ukraine, then the CIA's John Brennan and the FBI's James Comey would've been texting Putin our launch codes.

It's a dumb question. It's even a dumber one when you figure what might have happened if Trump were still president. Would that war even have occurred?

Trump is a pacifist, but in a particularly calculating way: he thinks war is a waste of blood and money. Which it often is, actually. There are worse ways of looking at these things.

My guess is he would have met with both parties and figured out a deal.

Would it have worked? I give it fifty-fifty—but I didn't think he'd be able to handle North Korea or facilitate the Abraham Accords, either. So what do I know? I thought the Abraham Accords were the new Hondas, until Dana explained it to me.

Fact is, Trump is so profoundly nonideological that he had no team (he is us). So he might have seen that our meddling in these affairs between two close (in at least two variables) countries made all of this worse.

Now, when Covid first broke out, Donald Trump used the war metaphor. We're fighting a disease, but it's no different than war. This was to get America to see that we're in this thing together, as if it were possible to share a foxhole with Nancy Pelosi and Rashida Tlaib. So now it seems we can use Covid as an analogy for war.

Do we want the illness to spread? But also, do we want a war to turn into a world war? Do the wrong thing and war can spread faster than that rash I keep getting when I don't wipe down my old ThighMaster. Here's the challenge.

It's always great when we aren't fighting the war—even when we are. You can send the money to those fighting and hope for the best. Now that's what you call <u>social distancing</u>!

Who's behind it? The weirdest and most hypocritical group since they shut down CNN+. It's weird to see all those folks who despised George W. Bush and Dick Cheney for Iraq now agreeing with (and even employing) their former staffers, as they push for a war that could in fact explode across the globe.

Meanwhile, you have noted antiwar legends admitting who's really antiwar these days. In a recent interview, famous lefty Noam Chomsky (yes, that Noam Chomsky) said that former president Trump was the one guy who could have solved the Ukrainian conflict—which is a little like Michael Moore penning a sonnet about Pilates.

In his own words, Chomsky said "fortunately" there is "one Western statesman of stature" who is pushing for a sensible solution to the crisis in Ukraine rather than looking for ways to fuel and prolong it. "His name is Donald J. Trump." Noam Chomsky, the socialist godfather of the Left, cites Donald Trump as suggesting an actual solution for Ukraine, which included more negotiations and diplomacy, not escalation.

Meanwhile, you have celebrities who will say you should pay more to support Ukraine. Who's the "you" in this? Truckers, salesmen, Uber drivers. This is the same detached mentality that we found with shut-downs. The rich can handle it, so why can't you?

Flipping Apathy into Energy

When Tony would yell my last name into my ear—it reminded me that I had come to play, and I'd better get my act together. It reminded me to forget everything that clouded my brain and get in the moment. And that somewhere out there in the ether, there were hundreds of thousands of people—some drunk, some high, some both—who were expecting me to surprise them. And that became my mission statement.

To surprise you.

I remember how each *Red Eye* show would begin: I felt that

same feeling all of you have when doing something that could end in disaster, simply because you were doing it in front of others. It was like losing your virginity, every night in front of a crowd. It's like the first time you peed in a trough at a MLB game or tried to kidnap a kid at the mall. It's like doing a wedding toast every single night.

I wasn't just unnerved by the viewers—but the crew. They were in that room, and I didn't want to embarrass myself in front of them either. I also had the show's guests . . . and the bigger they were, the more my anxiety would take hold. I didn't want to flounder in front of people I admired, or people who lowered themselves to join me that night.

I had no idea that the guests often felt the same way. Even big stars would get drunk before the show, to deal with their own anxiety. Then we'd meet at the table, and it would end disastrously, which made the show even more absurdly charming. (You should've seen Mick and Keith swigging vodka in the greenroom!) I've had comics on coke, actors boozed up, and talking heads mumbling through nicotine-derived panic attacks—if only you knew.

I did this thing every night straight for eight years or so. I know I was having fun, but I don't *remember* having that much fun—which is something I will never let happen again.

(That goes for colonoscopies, too).

<u>I will never let anxiety steal the joy from my life again</u> (which, I know, is a promise I know I can't keep forever).

I remember the anxiety more than the joy. But that would change. I would now enjoy the show as a viewer, and do what the viewer wanted—which helped me with *The Five*, and then *Gutfeld!* Once I made that commitment, I found happiness in my work, and un-assholed myself. A lot of this went all the way back to Tony shouting "Gutfeld!" into my ear. Because the enthusiasm behind that yell was the only thing that should matter. Not my insecurities, or all that anxious baggage around me.

So the exclamation stays . . . it's my way of telling me to get my mind right, and also to prepare you for a twisted steamroller. Which the show has become. Fox embraced the title in the end (and it all worked out for them because the show became such a huge hit!).

The exclamation point tells me that life is exciting, and this *is* exciting—and you had better fucking get ready and excited for it. This *is not* a chore. This is the best thing you could be doing in your life. And don't forget it. It's not just a kick in the ass. It's a kick in my ass. From the person best qualified to deliver it: me. (Well, actually my wife is best qualified, but she wears heels, and they hurt.) You can do this in your life too. And you'll be pleasantly surprised where that can take you.

Where Did the Critics Go?
They Flipped from Noisy to Silent

It's an interesting phenomenon. If the show had bombed, I think the criticism would be not just that I wasn't funny, but that right-wingers can't be funny, ever. Before the show even began, that was the mainstream criticism, from people who feel a joke needs to be deemed acceptable before they can laugh at it. How could people believe that anyway? You ever see Barry Goldwater's "Tijuana wedgie" routine? YouTube that.

But the show *didn't* bomb, so we'll never know (he said smugly).

Instead, it exploded like a bomb, quickly crushing the time slot. In mere weeks, collateral damage from that bomb included every show on CNN and MSNBC, whose numbers we crushed. Its ratings bested every show on CNN and MSNBC, our news rivals, and not just at the 11 p.m. hour when we aired—we bested every damn single hour of their programming. (Yeah, I know, I know . . . low bar. But still. That's pretty good for a new show.)

When the show premiered, the reviews from mainstream media were scathing, written by angry and emotionally scarred critics. Vice called it sickly . . . which was funny coming from a media company that had abandoned their once-daring editorial for a woke, criminally unfunny version of its former self. The real vice is how they've become a parrot of a gender studies course. And now they're bankrupt.

The *New Republic* said it was the worst show on television.

The best review came from *Variety*, written by a frazzled mess named Daniel D'Addario. I would suggest you google it for sheer comedic hilarity, but here's its hilarious prediction: "'Gutfeld!' fails as shareable comedy for the same reason it will likely run for as long as its star is willing to stumble through the TelePrompTer: Because it serves as a concentrated dose of Fox News at its most toxic."

Yes, it fails as "shareable comedy," as the audience grows and ends up becoming number one in the prized advertising demo in all of TV at 11 p.m.

I guess if I'm toxic, that means all those viewers are also toxic. And this helpless sap would likely agree.

But predictably, that's the last thing the guy ever wrote about the show, and not because I asked Tyrus to pay him a visit with a tire iron and Kat with some of her cooking.

Nope—he couldn't revisit it, that's why. It succeeded, and he failed. It was too much for him. It's like finding out the thing you hate has won, and you're still living in a studio apartment in Los Feliz writing angry missives for *Variety*.

The most hilarious trend: watching the media discussing the lack of "crucial representational" diversity among late night shows, especially with Samantha Bee and something called *Desus & Mero* being canceled. They ran through the late-night landscape, and could not mention the elephant in the Serengeti.

It wasn't just an elephant, it was a giant black intimidating man and a bony libertarian female—Tyrus and Kat—and they were as diverse as they come; more popular and edgy than any or all of these so-called other diverse, obscure voices combined. Yet Tyrus and Kat went ignored by these nobodies—because they were at Fox. It's funny how Fox became the true resting place for the risk-takers while places like Comedy Central and Vice ended up as graveyards for diversity hires—destroying their own brands in the name of wokeness.

On top of that, we made mincemeat of the late-night comedy shows, because we were fearlessly saying whatever the hell we wanted. They couldn't do that; we could. Fox was the true terrain of free speech. There is nothing like my show on television. And that's why their shows are dying, and mine isn't. Well, also, those other shows blow.

Kat and Tyrus never ever self-censor. It's funny: when I might think that maybe I went too far on something, they would rise to the occasion and better me.

You could not find a better pair of people to save your ass every night.

Because the show is a success, it's hard to argue with my idiosyncrasies—even though they are real and should be questioned by psychiatrists and other mental health professionals—although God knows they're not doing that to the violent thugs wandering New York City sidewalks.

But the funniest thing about the critics: they think I am appealing to an audience, when actually I'm risking everything I have with the audience every night. Here's why.

The Left Embraces Force, the Right Fights It

In a *Los Angeles Times* piece on how late-night comedians covered the January 6 hearings, all the shows the *Times* covered featured the exact same response, in unison.

The *Times* mysteriously left off one show. Now, what show could that be? Yep, the Gutfeld show. The number one show somehow didn't merit the same interest as the others it had trounced.

So why would they do that? Why leave out this gorgeous little show (with this gorgeous little host)?

I believe it's part of a shift, where instead of speaking truth to power, the media and their cherished comics must align themselves with it or lose their prized pedestal. In my opinion, that makes them left-wing advocates as much as comedians.

Previously, they would find outrage and humor in the government going after protesters.

Especially protesters who might in fact be truly protesting—and not looting and burning down buildings.

Instead, they embraced the side of those doing the persecuting—sorry, prosecuting.

We didn't do that on my show. Instead we made fun of the inquisitors. Like the bitter emotional scolds Liz Cheney and Adam Kinzinger. These are two sweaty, fretting neocons, mind you, that the modern Left now embraces. Talk about a flip. Wait until the hearings are over. These two are going to learn how much the Left really loves them. Answer: not so much.

The Cheney family gave us two wars—one based on a lie that led to the deaths of hundreds of thousands of people. The idea that somehow Liz Cheney is considered a hero to liberals, a woman who rejected her sister's own same-sex marriage while defending the upheaval of *Roe v. Wade*, is richer than her old man from Halliburton.

But it's a calculated flip. The Left is using her to hit Republicans, a party she belongs to—and she's too stupid to see it.

On my show we bucked the conformity, and said our peace usually on behalf of the protesters, while always condemning those who broke the law. In fact, unlike Democrats during the post–George Floyd riots, we actually wanted *all* lawbreakers punished, whether you burned down a pawnshop or stole Pelosi's podium. And as much as we sympathized with MAGA supporters, we weren't going to bail 'em out.

Even if they deserved it.

But the real flip is the one no one is talking about.

Imagine a female, unarmed protester was shot dead by the cops as she tried to enter a building. Imagine if she were Antifa, or Black Lives Matter or a pro-choice, or a Pussy-hat-wearing granny?

You would know her name, date of birth, favorite color, and who she took to the prom.

More important, you would know even more about the cop.

Because the media, and liberal media in particular, loves to martyr protesters—even armed ones who initiate violence.

But here? Ashli Babbitt? They denigrated her. They laughed at her.

The Left found an unarmed protester whose death they could defend and even relish, one who, rightly or wrongly, believed she was saving the country from internal corruption. She wasn't trying to overthrow democracy, but was trying to protect it; she might have been wrong—but since when is that a capital crime worthy of death? I'll tell you when. Since Biden and his handlers moved into the White House.

Talk about a flip.

If a cop was involved in shooting a black suspect, every lib demanded to know the cop's name, whether the cop was in the wrong or not.

But after the shooting of Babbitt in the Capitol on January 6, 2021, the cop's identity, background, and work history remained shrouded for months. The anti-cop left, fresh from pushing to defund the police, now were creating a human shield around one D.C. cop, who happened to be black by the way, who shot dead an unarmed white woman.

The Left made a joke out of it. Suddenly they sounded like long-ago Birmingham, Alabama, police chief Bull Connor referring to blacks. "You know, if you don't want to get shot, don't break the law" was the summary explanation for her death. "Play dangerous games, win dangerous prizes," said folks who previously would have defended perps with guns shooting at cops. The same folks who praised protesters burning down federal buildings in Portland, Oregon, now supported shooting a protester just for *entering* a federal building.

Speaking truth to power became dropping to your knees to pleasure armed authority. Does the Columbia School of Journalism issue knee pads at graduation?

Look what happened when the Dems introduced a new spending bill that also included money for the hiring of more than eighty thousand IRS agents.

Democrats went from defending the little guy to cheerleading their adversary—a massive posse of government-sanctioned police whose only job is to make your life so difficult you fork over your money rather than fight.

On Fox News, Mike Emanuel asked Democrat Senator Ben Cardin of Maryland a basic question: "Can you understand how eighty-seven thousand new IRS agents would scare the heck out of millions of Americans?" The senator replied, coldly, "If there's no reason to be fearful, and if you paid your taxes and if you complied with our laws, you should want to make sure everyone else does that." Can you imagine Ted Cruz or any prominent Republican saying that about a black man being roughed up by a cop? "Hey, if you don't wanna get hurt, just comply with our laws." Never mind that our tax laws are so complicated and arbitrary, Alan Dershowitz, Stephen Hawking, and the Mensa membership couldn't tell you how to file safely every time.

What about having to hire an accountant or a lawyer to help defend your case of this arbitrary audit? (I say arbitrary, but I might be giving the IRS too much credit.) That's something you should embrace because it means they're also catching really bad people, while checking up on you. In a way you should be thanking them for their audit, sort of like telling a mugger, "Thank you, sir, may I have another."

You want to watch this flip in real time?

Here's IRS agent Adam Markowitz, considered by *Forbes* one of the top one hundred "must-follows" among tax Twitter accounts. He arrogantly educated America that the new massive army of IRS agents Biden proposed to police us more diligently is no real concern! Unless you're guilty. This is something you heard from J. Edgar Hoover.

Justifying this new army, Markowitz says, "All of my GOP friends who are worried about 87,000 IRS agents coming after the little guy . . . how about just don't cheat on tax returns? A fully truthful and accurate tax return is bulletproof in an audit. I never understood the fear of an IRS audit." Right, because *you're* a fucking accountant.

No, Adam, here's two words for you: Lois Lerner.

So yeah, to all you white liberal friends and criminals . . . how about just don't rape, rob, and break the law. A life lived honestly, and crime-free, acts as a bulletproof vest when dealing with the cops.

I guess Adam never heard of the presumption of innocence, but I suppose I'm the idiot on that one: here, it's different. You get the call from the IRS, and it's up to you to prove you're innocent. Because you aren't charged with anything—yet. That's the grift.

Upon realizing his idiocy, this agent admits in a later tweet:

"I get that it's a headache to go through an audit. Nobody wants to do that. And I get that it's costly to go through an audit and nobody ever wins when an audit comes calling."

Wait a second, you jackass—you just said no one should fear an audit, and then moments later explain exactly why they should fear it? That it disrupts your life, puts the onus (and anus) on you to clear your name even though you've done nothing wrong. And you say that it's good for the country? And we're supposed to trust this jackass? Fuck him and the audit he rode in on!

So you can shoot unarmed women, target anyone you want for audits, and you get a cheerleading squad on your behalf— a squad you saw in full force when it came to mask mandates, lockdowns, and vaccination regulations.

Generally you'd think that this would be stuff of right-wing wet dreams. We love a good dose of law and order! We long for the old days of "might makes right!" We cherish fascism, as our media overlords would tell us.

Yet, what happened? The loudest voices for real freedom were *on the right*.

The ones preaching government control were *on the left*.

And boy, did this flip everything upside down.

Suddenly, old rockers like Van Morrison and Eric Clapton became true radicals, but bands like Rage Against the Machine, who cosplay as revolutionaries (while raking in millions from aging bald liberals of both sexes), embraced government rule. Rage Against the Machine? More like We Are the Machine.

The new fascism comes to the tune of shitty music, apparently.

The flip was camouflaged. The supporters of draconian lockdown policies could say, "Look, it's not the government sanctioning this! It's private businesses," leaving out the obvious point that if businesses don't comply they get shut down. So the government deputized fellow citizens to be the cops in the pandemic, and the Left happily applauded—even as their leaders violated such policies daily and flagrantly.

In sum, they forced it on companies—who then act as the enforcement arm for the government. The Dems can say, "No one is telling you to wear a mask or get a shot," but good luck entering any place without a mask or a vaccine card. The Left made all the old suit-wearing corporate types into narcs. Another flip.

As I write this, I still have friends who aren't allowed in the building to do their work. But it's not Fox's fault. It's the government who creates laws that put the responsibility on them to enforce them. Or they get screwed or sued. Gee, might this administration want to take shots at Fox News?

We are a nation now run by lawyers. Not leaders. And it's the Left that cheers it on. Even Libertarians fell off their chosen path.

The people who normally say, "Live and let live," became, "How dare you try to kill me with your maskless face!" And let's face it: Libertarians are generally either Republicans who like to take drugs, or Democrats who've been arrested. In this case, it was generally the latter.

I understand that we all obey laws that limit our freedoms. We wear seat belts—an obvious example; but that's mainly to protect yourself.

There is a happy midpoint—but it was one that the formerly freedom-loving left chose to ignore. It was all or nothing, in their opinion.

So you had the Centers for Disease Control and Prevention (CDC) saying, despite the science saying otherwise, that masks were still needed on public transportation—yet the media and left blindly applauded it. Hosts on MSNBC would trash a judge who sided with getting rid of masks on airlines, while gushing over those who demanded that masks stay in place. *New York Times* columnist Paul Krugman predicted there would be violence against mask wearers once the mandate was lifted. Yes, because if we don't like something, we express it through violence—unlike the people who vote like he does, who showed such restraint after the Floyd death. Meanwhile, he supports a president who tells Americans it's pointless to own a gun, because the government has F-15s. You know, the administration whose vice president supported a fund to bail out rioting protesters.

Are you getting the point? These lefties are dumb fascist motherfuckers, which, by the way, used to be the Right's moniker, so count that as another flip.

(Another odd flip: the media applauded violent protest for two years—then claimed the Right is better at it and it's terrible, apparently.)

The Mask Mandates

It wasn't just the IRS that decided more power was necessary to keep a free society from being "too free." Suddenly we now had a new victim class, and it wasn't taxpayers being targeted by agents. It was "the masked"!

The CDC fell victim to an essential reaction that happens whenever your power grows. You get used to it. You don't want it to go away. Once you start a war, ending it seems unnecessary, especially when you're immune to the oppressive rules that you yourself put in place.

Look at Vietnam or Afghanistan. They went on well past

the public's desire for war. Meanwhile, the Patriot Act has more extensions than a dining room table at Mitt Romney's house. Look at the drug war. It's a war that creates more casualties than it prevents. Yet it rolls along, racking up more deaths than Covid ever could.

Covid is another war that those in power wish would stick around because it gives them authority. As *Politico* points out, public health and legal experts worry it could diminish their power over public health. No wonder the media reacted to the end of the mask mandate with terror. *It meant an end to their authority to tell you what to do.* Dr. Anthony Fauci would have to go back to his Hobbit cave and mix his "novel" potions without an audience. So in response they referred to the maskless as assholes, as they prepared for hate crimes against the masked, who are now part of the constellation of the oppressed. A box to be ticked. A new protected class. Let's refund their college loans. But only the masked!

Yes, I am masked. I am a true rebel, for every part of my identity gets a seal of approval from the media. True rebellion, flipped into true conformity.

It's not like people are saying you can't wear a mask, by the way.

Because it's more about the people in power forcing you to wear one, while they *don't*. Remember the Met Gala—what a truly gorgeous example of the flip: where our nation's most vocal progressives prance about, maskless in gorgeous gowns, while the servants, on their knees dealing with the unmasked needs, must be fully masked. The servants: masked. The leaders: unmasked. It's a reminder that for the Left it's always about status and class distinctions, not race. Although, race as an inflection point hides their own class hatred. And galas. They do love a gala.

Credit: AP Images

Hilariously, they defend your right to wear a mask, the same way they defended women in Islamic countries to wear burkas. It's actually worse—because it wasn't a "some people can wear a mask and some don't have to," the way it was with often falsely portrayed burkas. It was *everyone has to wear a mask*. Or you want old people dead. Yes, in many Islamic countries, if you didn't wear a burka, you'd be beaten or worse. But instead of the Left saying women should be free not to wear a burka, they said they should be free to wear one. They were all for face burkas and they call it freedom. Well, I'll do the same the next time I tie up a hitchhiker.

This sort of mask militancy was intoxicating. It gave power to people who rarely get to feel it. You'd be sitting in a packed flight, and an attendant would treat you like Josef Mengele if your mask slipped below one nostril. If you tried to explain that it was an accident, they would scold you not to talk back—that you have been warned, and if you do it again, you will put you on a list (this actually happened to me). This takes place in an environment where advanced filtration systems remove nearly all airborne contamination. Hell, maybe we should make all rooms like airplane cabins. The air on a plane is cleaner than the air in whatever city you're flying to. You can bet that much.

But the press ignored all that, even making up science as they went along—saying that a person sneezing a few rows up from you could give your family the flu (a Joe Scarborough classic; and you didn't even see Mika Brzezinski's lips move).

The fact is, in this flipped world, the only thing that was really contagious was a peculiar thirst for power. Not global power—but intimate, super, local power. The kind the classroom monitor enjoys. Snoopy, tattletale, sanctimonious power. As humans, let's face it: we get bored with our own limitations. The thought of affecting other lives is exciting. It doesn't take much to turn a neighbor into an informer, if they get a dopamine hit of authority, of power.

It's where you can exact punishment on the people closest around you. So it pits the crew against the customers, hostesses against regular paying diners, neighbors who share elevators with you. Imagine coming home after a long day of work to have some double-masked tenant lecture you on health in your elevator ride up. If you ever find yourself in that exact situation, just point to the maximum-weight-limit sign in the elevator and say, "You're putting my life at risk right now so let's call it a draw."

Technically, if they can lecture me on masks, I should be able to lecture them on their chronic obesity, which is not only a burden on their hearts, but also on our economy, and the elevator I'm currently sharing with them.

The flip also reveals why people get into politics. It's always to allow them the exemption of the rules they enforce on others. So while Barack Obama was extolling the virtues of masks and lockdown, he invited five hundred people to his sixtieth birthday party at his $12 million mansion. I think it was near the beach—so apparently he's not worried about the rising sea levels caused by climate change, either.

By the way, I salute Obama for living his best life in the pandemic. But the message he was sending, of course, was only meant for him, and people like him. You know if a loved one of his was dying, he'd be able to see them. But not *you*. At least when Russians have oligarchs, they call them that.

You see, Washington, D.C., mayor Muriel Bowser was once photographed maskless at a wedding reception right after reinstating the mask mandate. So, there she was indulging in the behavior she banned for others. But I get it—how can you do a macarena conga line when you're six feet apart, wearing a mask? Did the groom kiss the bride through a mask? The only social distancing going on at a wedding is usually the in-laws hiding from each other.

But Bowser said the city would reimpose indoor mask mandates regardless of vaccine status—a thoroughly antiscience move. This was in a city that averaged one Covid death a week during that time. I think she might have said, "Let them eat cake!" And a few people yelled back, "We can't, we're wearing a fucking mask!"

Then there was the policy bulletin announcing that if any visitor or staff failed to comply at Capitol Hill over masks they would be arrested for unlawful entry. You know who was missing in that threat? The politicians. It was just "staffers and visitors."

Chicago mayor Lori Lightfoot attended the "superspreader event" Lollapalooza, featuring bands that no one remembers—despite threatening new lockdowns if Covid cases rose.

Yet Fauci told Americans that masks must be worn.

So, why are the leaders enforcing the laws on the law abiders, but not anyone else? It seems like pure cowardice. It also raises the question: Can Fauci and Lightfoot go back to the Lollipop Guild already?

Have they ever actually been to a homeless encampment in downtown Los Angeles and asked them why they aren't in masks? Or is it just easier to yell at you instead of at them? (The answer is yes.)

But it's funny. Imagine pulling a fire alarm, then all the fire trucks go to a place where there is no fire.

That's what you get from political leaders who are more inflamed about the unmasked than they are about violent transients on subways or smash-and-grabbers in Walgreens. It's like the old joke of losing your eyeglasses in the bedroom but looking in the kitchen because the lighting is better. God, I miss Emo Philips!

Again, I return to Gutfeld's golden rule: one enters politics to become immune to the laws one creates for others. It's their vaccine against limits to their freedoms. And it's only available to them—not you.

So you have "medical experts" in the media calling on the

FBI to target Americans sharing "misinformation" about vaccines. They demand a concerted effort at the federal level to combat misinformation. This is about holding social media platforms responsible, they say, using cybersecurity and the FBI. Some even describe opponents of mask mandates as white nationalist anarchists. An MSNBC panel claimed parents who protested against mask mandates at their kids' public schools were influenced by white supremacy.

You had people being denied transplants because they weren't vaccinated.

Never mind that during the height of this weirdness, the most vax-reluctant groups were young black and Hispanic people—which makes white supremacy the most diverse group of people since "It's a Small World." The Left does this thing where if two people share an interest, they are in cahoots. Do you think climate change data is unreliable? Well, so did Alex Jones. Did you vote for Trump? So did O. J. Simpson! Of course this can work both ways—the absurd one: Hitler was a vegetarian, and Stalin loved Maroon 5, so if white power types are suspicious of the government and the vaccine, and Larry Elder feels the same—ergo etc.! Everyone is now a white supremacist.

You might think college students would come out against mandates untethered to science. But you'd be wrong.

College students in Iowa, of all places, actually staged a "die-in" protesting that they wanted *more* Covid policies on campus, not less. Good thing we're paying for their student loans, eh? America's future leaders.

Think about that as a flip.

Maybe thirty years ago, students would protest meaningful stuff, like for free speech and against war, right or wrong—big stuff. They used to burn bras, but now they wear them on their faces.

The best part of this: the pro-mask protest was organized by the "Campaign to Organize Graduate Students," or COGS. A pretty accurate acronym for these mindless twerps. I still hope it was a prank.

There is a new kind of ideology brewing—and it's a mix of old ones. For now, I would call it the *ideology of punishment.* There's something addictive about telling people how to live their lives. But it's incorporated identity politics—it's white people who won't obey, and it's the Left who wear their masks like flags. People love telling other people what to do and how to live, and identity politics allows one segment to shame them over a past (they had no part in), so they will ultimately do what you say—whether it's fly a BLM flag, wear a rainbow pin, or watch more than one dreadful episode of *This Is Us.*

Meanwhile, NPR developed a system to snitch on coworkers who aren't complying with the very pro-mask-wearing policies. They encourage others to rat 'em out.

Of course, this is something that, again, they would condemn the Right for—the key term always being *McCarthyism*. But they've really mastered it here. It was used to force medicine into people—which is a far more intense practice than going after people for communist leanings. They are actually targeting people who, for good reason or bad, don't want to be forced to put something into their bodies that they don't believe has been thoroughly vetted.

It's weird how the Left embraced lockdowns. The science wasn't good to the lockdowns. Studies compared how well states handled the pandemic. Turns out the ones that came out worse had the toughest lockdowns and policies.

This is according to the Committee to Unleash Prosperity, which graded the states by comparing deaths, economies, and impact on education. They found that the bottom ten were dominated by states with the most severe lockdowns and among the last to finally reopen schools. They found that shutting down economies and schools was by far the biggest mistake officials and leaders made during Covid, especially among blue states.

Yet who did they make the hero of Covid? Governor Andrew Cuomo of New York, who, before his downfall, was pegged by the drooling media as the next leader of the free world. Some even assumed he was acting president during Covid, not the current dude in office.

They even created a fan base for him—the Cuomosexual.

If you were one of them, I hope you got monkeypox. Sorry, Cuomopox.

New York actually performed poorly on every measure, ranking forty-ninth overall, according to C.U.P. Which is generally where New York ranks on everything these days.

True, we did bump up our numbers of people getting shoved off subway platforms, well-staged group looting, mass shooters, and street poopers. New Jersey, whose state bird is asbestos, was the worst-performing state, the study found. Fact is, the only people who benefited from wearing masks were the criminals smashing and grabbing luxury brands in SoHo. They couldn't be recognized. Plus, they didn't have to smell New Jersey. It got so bad, even the mayor of NYC—an actual Democrat—pleaded with business owners to now <u>ban</u> people from <u>wearing masks</u> in their stores!

Who topped the list? Utah, Nebraska, Vermont, and Florida—which are all governed by Republicans. But states that locked down businesses, churches, schools, and restaurants for lengthy periods <u>did not</u> have lower death rates than those that remained open. Arguably the freest state in the union, Florida, got shit from the so-called progressives for being, well, too free. Do you remember "DeathSantis," a moniker that showed how the Left really lost their flair for ridicule? Yet Florida did away with Covid restrictions early on and ranked almost no different than California in terms of deaths. You can say, wow, no big difference—California was ranked twenty-seventh in deaths, Florida twenty-eighth. But that's the point.

Florida not locking down still did better than the most locked-down state—and they did it with a population's age that approaches a Galápagos tortoise. Meanwhile, California's governor was partying at the Napa Valley restaurant called, pretentiously, the French Laundry while families were stuck in solitary confinement.

Who knew the smoked quail appetizer had such protective powers? At this point, Newsom would have to send his governorship to ten laundries to erase this stain of entitled, sneering elitism.

While research shows that keeping schools closed had no impact on the number of deaths in kids or adults—the school boards are still wearing masks—I guess that's so we can't see them laughing at us.

Ironically, those demanding we follow the science did the worst. I guess they meant the political science. The lesson: The people who accuse you of not caring, of having blood on your hands or putting Grandma at risk, were the ones guilty of all three. I think shrinks call that projecting—vomiting their sins on you.

The Flip: I'm Not Joining Fox; Fox Is Joining Me

I stated this in the previous book: I would never join your group to become more like the group. I joined your group so they would become more like me. I think I stole that motto from Tony Robbins or Tony Danza, I can't remember which.

This applies to fraternities, the Republican Party, the gym, the knitting circle at the local church, and of course Fox News.

Fox is a way different place now than it was then. I'm not saying it's all due to me. I'm saying that I showed them that content can take different forms. In my case, it can come across, at first, as something opposite what they might want.

I could not have started working there and morphed into Bill O'Reilly or Glenn Beck. That's not me. But being at Fox now for roughly fifteen years, I've seen the company move incrementally closer to me, while maintaining its true vision, which is one that I've always embraced.

There are some things you see now at Fox you would never have seen before me.

1. Me

2. Tyrus and Timpf.

3. That thing Bill Hemmer can do with his duodenum.

You would not see the cross-pollination of hosts and panelists making fun of each other—a teasing component that doesn't exist anywhere else. You never saw Don Lemon calling Anderson Cooper a preening Q-tip. You don't see Rachel Maddow pointing out that she could beat Chris Hayes in arm wrestling. (Hell, Dana could beat Chris Hayes in arm wrestling.)

But on Fox, you see me ridiculing Brian Kilmeade. You see Judge Jeanine Pirro ripping me. You see Jesse Watters making fun of my musical taste to make up for his shoddy hairpiece, while Dana Perino points out my height (shortly before being given a stepping stool to reach her chair). We make fun of each other's shows, our clothes, our hair, our lyric poetry.

If you can't do that, it means you truly don't get along.

A family that teases together, stays together. I think that was Charlie Manson's quote under his yearbook picture in high school.

Here's a scientific study I did on my own time: a lot of the people who have left Fox (I won't roll through the names) were incapable of being teased. In fact, one anchor, during a break, actually asked me not to make jokes about him. It was awkward and strange: it's like he was asking me to not be his friend. Maybe that was exactly what he was asking—I wasn't anyway, so it wasn't a problem. But if you can't handle it, then it's a sign that you take yourself too seriously. As it turns out, no one could take him seriously enough anyway. (And folks . . . that man's name was Walter Cronkite.)

You also see topics that wouldn't be covered a certain way until my merry band of miscreants showed up. I talk about my stance on drug legalization (which I am for); Kat proclaims her pro stance on sex work. These are things you'd usually never see on Fox, or for any other network for that matter. What makes the success of the Gutfeld show more amazing is that we are doing comedy on a news network! And not just any news network—the number one news network in all of news! News networks aren't and haven't been ever known for their senses of humor. In fact, they are some of the stuffiest, most PC terrains on the planet. That why I give the upper brass at FNC all the credit for . . . well, having brass ones. They respect speech more than most cliched "outspoken" comics.

We also bring out the real life humanity of Foxers who come on my show.

Whether it's Dagen McDowell, Dana Perino, or Brian Kilmeade, the constant roasting of guests makes them more real than anyone else in entertainment. You get to know them.

You now know more about them than lesser members of your own family (you know who I'm talking about). It's why when people talk to us on the street, they act like they know us so well that they start in on conversations as if they've known us for years.

I gotta get better security. You people are *annoying*.

Mainly because we are you. And you are us. If that sounds like bullshit, it's only because the entertainment industry created an idea that *they* were different.

They are, perhaps. But only because they're a fucking mess.

Fans might ask for selfies, but it's usually after they want to talk about last night's show and why I was wrong about student loans, or opioids, or Geraldo's mustache (I believe it's actually a sleeping caterpillar that holds his face together).

But, when I am approached by fans, I get the same question over and over again: How do I stay in such great shape? But also, how did I get away with this? And should a federal task force be formed in response?

It's the most important question in my life. I'm going to answer it finally in this book.

How I Got Away with This

This question isn't really just about the success of my new show, or *The Five*, or *Red Eye*—it's about how I managed to survive and thrive on this planet—to make it through this entire life relatively unscathed while being not just a moral theorist but a practical degenerate. In every stage, people who have observed my behavior ask the same thing: "How does this jackass always get away with it?"

Even in my teens, it was a constant curiosity. I was given a wide berth among friends and family to do what I do. Maybe it was because I had a sick dad, but I wonder if it had more to do with having a sick mind.

True, I would get suspended from school and even in one case expelled (then allowed to return, which I guess is actually suspended, but with better street cred), but I learned, perhaps from my mom, that I if I said the unspeakable truths with a smile and a laugh, then it would dull the impact of what I said. As the intimidating hulk of a comic Nick Di Paolo said to me, "Damn, I should have smiled more."

But my offensiveness was more about inclusivity than the opposite. I was never trying to hurt anyone; I was trying to find some commonality, by saying the quiet stuff lurking in our brains, out loud. Problem was, my personality didn't come with an owner's manual for others. I could understand it, but that was about it—at least until I got older.

Fighting the Bully [That Bully Was Me]

My bizarre sensibilities didn't always work on my behalf. When I was younger—say in second or third grade—and I could actually find a new best friend, I would relentlessly tease them. I had no idea that this ruthless behavior was not a good thing. I thought it was the way to communicate lovingly to people you really, really liked. The ones I really, really, really liked, I would try to push into traffic.

It's like your high school football coach not yelling at you. It's not because he likes you more. It's just the opposite. He thinks you stink and have no potential. So why waste his breath on you? In the long run he doesn't see you being of any use to him or the team. By the way, the analogy is courtesy of Nick Di Paolo, since he really sucked at football.

The Decrepit Exemption

During my teenage years, I would go on summer vacations with a buddy's family, a pretty traditional and religious bunch. There were a bunch of brothers, and none of them swore. They all went to church. Together. None of them made sick jokes. If they did, they would be admonished. But for some reason, I could show up at their house and none of their parents' rules applied to me.

I could say mostly anything I pleased . . . In fact, it was encouraged. By their parents, no less!

I would make a joke about using babies as skeet targets at the firing range, and his mom and dad would say, "Oh, that Greg!" It became a recurring joke among everyone. "Oh, that Greg."

That was one made-up example—but this happened in nearly every household. In the evening, the parents would prefer to hang out with me and listen to my bizarre opinions and they would laugh and laugh. I had leeway that they wouldn't afford any family member. I realized that this is also how people viewed my mother.

I think they gave her some leeway because "she's got that son on her hands, who should probably be put to sleep."

In any case, maybe that leeway was because the unrelated people could enjoy the risk of me without such deviance reflecting on their parenting. If perhaps I was their kid, they would treat me differently.

I could have been grounded or thrown out of the house. Instead, the parents would laugh and go, "Oh that Greg!" It was like when an unexpected sex scene comes on in a movie you're watching with your in-laws. You're blameless, even if you enjoy it.

That became a pattern in my life. I could say things other people couldn't say or would find offensive—but they would excuse me for it. And find themselves amused by it.

It's one thing to be the class clown in school (which I was and maybe you were, too), but it's another to be the class clown and having the teacher cracking up so he can't punish you. It helped that I had pictures of most of them passed out in my treehouse.

They Called Her "Jackie"

I remember being ashamed of the fact that my parents were older. I saw my mother as unstable and angrily emotional. She would say things off the top of her head that would be shocking and downright mean. (I still remember when she said FDR was the worst sitting president ever.) There was no way I was going to invite my friends over to my house—God knows what she might say to them. I preferred to go to my friend's house, and not the reverse.

But at one point I relented, and some classmates stopped by.

Then they started coming by more and more.

When they would come, they wouldn't leave. In retrospect, the fact that I had three sisters might have had something to do with it. But not really.

It definitely had nothing to do with me—it had to do with my mom. My friends liked her more than they liked me. They still do, and she passed away eight years ago. It became extremely obvious when I would come home to see my mom, and my friends were in the living room with her, drinking beer. I would say hello, and they would acknowledge my presence—then return to their own hell-raising. They didn't even bother telling me they were coming over. They were just stopping by to talk to "Jackie." Yeah, they called her Jackie.

I learned a few things from this.

One, you might be wrong in how you judge people. In fact, you are almost always wrong, as they are wrong about you. I looked at my mom the way some people looked at me: mean, snarky, even vicious. But it turned out she was just me playing at a level that had been her forte for six decades. She made Don Rickles look like Oral Roberts.

I realized later that I could make Jackie my secret weapon. I started to use her in *Men's Health* columns giving household tips (an irony, since she was a terrible house cleaner), then gave her a regular column at *Stuff* magazine, where she answered readers' questions about relationships, then when I got to TV, she got a nightly gig on *Red Eye*.

It was all purely by accident, really. I simply decided to call her up during the show and hooked it up to the studio sound, and it was magic. The old lady ended up being on the show merely every day of the week, mainly because it was the one segment that would be a surefire hit. Plus, we didn't have to pay her. I think I told her we would "take care of her down the line," or something like that.

Every night she came on via phone and ragged on me, in particular—with an honesty you wouldn't hear anywhere else. Sometimes it was cute, or shocking, but it was real. She'd call me filthy or admonish the female guests for their revealing wardrobe. There was no filter, although I could tell she wrote notes ahead of time—just like I do, probably with a Sharpie.

It worked. That was always my goal, but I had no idea I had an ally in my own family tree. To disarm people with surprise and truth—my mom did the trick.

It's exactly what I did on *Red Eye* (to cult success) and then *The Five* (to mainstream success) and then the weekly *Greg Gutfeld Show*, and now the nightly one with the happy exclamation point.

The inspiration for honesty and bluntness came from my mother. I think about her a lot more now that she's gone—and now that the show is basically a manifestation of her blunt but happy and sometimes wistful look at life. Wherever she is, she's got to be laughing, but also critical of my poop jokes and other naughty asides. She was never a fan of my dirty jokes—be they poop or boob related. I am sure she would probably have a problem with at least 10 to 20 percent of the content.

But she no doubt would get the exclamation point, because nearly everything she said ended in one.

The Fear of a Bigger Footprint

Roughly a decade ago, as *The Five* took off, I met with the top brass, and they floated the idea of a Gutfeld helming a Fox News version of *The Daily Show*, but without the annoying "Jon Stewart" part.

The idea would be that I would likely leave *The Five* at some point and do a comedy show, late at night, four times a week for a shit ton of money. I was minted. I was finally in the club! I was now one of the big boys—and surely my face would be on the sides of buildings, as opposed to interiors of post offices, or in a heart-shaped frame on Brian Stelter's nightstand. I would get a key to the executive washroom, my own parking space, and of course my own fully staffed omelet station in my office. (Every major anchor at Fox has one, and they're all manned by the same chef. His name . . . Chris Cuomo. I guess FNC felt bad when his career crashed like Anne Heche leaving a Jell-O shot contest.)

Well, that never happened. At least for a decade.

Mainly because there was no way I was leaving *The Five*. They wouldn't let me, and I also wouldn't let myself. The gig was too much fun, and I am always wary of leaving something that works. The show is amazing, the people are amazing, and their amazingness allowed me to be who I am, which is amazing!

Being among people like Dana and now Jesse, the Judge, Harold, Jessica, and Geraldo, allowed me to be who I was. Teasing Dana, and her affectionate, faux-offended responses, made my behavior more appealing. She was the girl who sat in front of me in sixth grade who took no offense at my jokes— instead she found them funny, and returned volleys that were equally impressive.

I think she saved me from being fired. By laughing at me. Maybe I shouldn't have written that. She'll probably stop laughing now. (No worries, though. She won't read the book—although she will say she *did*, and in one sitting! On a ten-minute ride in an Uber to her charity work with Ugandan refugees.)

Why You Should Flip Your Thinking: Look Forward to Being Fired (for the Right Reasons)

I prefer to be fired. It's just more dramatic, true—but it means you're never complacent.

I'd been fired three times before—twice by the same boss.

My first firing happened when I was editor of *Men's Health*—and it was a godsend, even though I didn't know it at the time.

Before I got canned, I remember my features editor, Mike Corcoran, coming to my office after reading my story on sex addiction, and he said one thing to me that stayed with me forever: "You have to get the hell out of here."

I knew what he meant, but I wasn't going to quit. At some point they were going to have to throw me out, because I was too fucking good at my job. And I really like staying where I'm at, even if there are better things on the horizon. I once sat in a restaurant I really liked for six weeks. I only left when it became a Jiffy Lube.

I loved the job—after all, I had been there for five years—but I was always butting heads with some severely humorless bosses. Not my great editors like Mike Lafavore or Mark Bricklin, but their bosses, who were confused by my frankness and angered at my mockery toward their new age hokum. (The owner of the company wasn't just a tree hugger, she was *literally* a tree hugger: she would go outside and get photographed hugging trees. This kind of unsolicited physical activity would not pass muster these days in a corporate setting. She was arborsexual before it was a thing.)

It didn't matter that I had edited and written the most successful pieces they would publish; nor did it matter that I made subject matter (health) that was naturally boring into something interesting. I might be the only writer who could make a colonoscopy sound like *Pirates of the Caribbean*. If you had my colon, you'd know what I mean.

But I also took risks that turned out to be too far ahead of their time.

When they saw the opportunity to unload me (after a commission I did on best colleges for men, a piece I didn't write or even edit), they did it. The story was deemed too critical of college diversity pushing, especially the college the CEO went to. I was twenty years ahead of my time—realizing that identity was replacing competence. The first step toward wokeism.

One afternoon I was called by human resources and told I was being "transitioned out." (Transitioned had a whole different meaning than it does today.)

They offered me a job as "editor at large" and slipped a paper in front of me that they wanted me to sign that approved of the move. Now, even I knew that "editor at large" meant "formerly important." Suddenly they wanted to turn me into the fat old guy hanging around the bar, ogling the bright young things. I started laughing and got up and left. I walked to my car and drove to my office and got my stuff to leave. The HR director followed me in his car and approached me in the parking lot and asked me if I was "okay." He looked scared. It was then that I realized they were terrified of me. I grabbed my bag and said nothing. I called a bunch of friends and coworkers and threw a raging party at my stone castle on Union Street in Allentown. I then dropped a line to the *New York Post* and returned fire.

The *Post* ran a piece on my firing, not simply because I was fired, but that afternoon I wrote an editorial letter and sent it along with the other pages of the magazine, where it ended up being printed in the monthly rag. It made it into tens of thousands of copies before they were able to stop the printing. It was a huge story: that a fired editor left a place in flames as he walked out the door. In the letter, I explained why I had been fired, and that it had to do with fear, and once you work with people who are terrified of you, it's over. The story went viral— a tough thing to do before we had Twitter. But it got picked up everywhere. And by sheer coincidence my health insurance was canceled, but was quickly reinstated after I dropped *that* story to the press.

The next day I got job offers from so many magazines I lost count—from mass-market women's mags to competing men's mags, including ones from England—so clearly other people got what I was doing, and wanted it badly. I went through the offers and settled on *Stuff* magazine, mainly because it was fresh, funny, honest, and open to malleability—and I really liked my boss, Andy Clerkson. Also, *Stuff*, as a title, could mean anything.

The brass at *Stuff* knew what I was up to and bought it completely. Which was their first mistake.

The Twitter Flip

Speaking of mistakes, let's observe insane media response over Elon Musk buying Twitter. First, let's listen to the dumbest take in the universe, from Ari Melber, who said, "I'm just telling you, this thing matters a ton. If you own all of Twitter or Facebook or what have you. You don't have to explain yourself. You don't even have to be transparent. You could secretly ban one party's candidate or all of its candidates, all of its nominees. Or you could just secretly turn down the reach of their stuff and turn up the reach of something else. And the rest of us might not even find out about it till after the election."

Exactly.

My God, where has this moron been? He just described how the Left has been using social media for ages: to push hoaxes, while burying real stories like Hunter Biden's laptop in order to change an election. In his own complaint, he just exposed the problem that Musk had aimed to solve. They're not afraid of what conservatives might do to them, but of what might be found out about them: they've been rigging the game, from day one.

Now you have the media claiming that defending free speech is simply another complaint from privileged white men. Where was all this privilege when I was growing up? Every time I got fired? (Three times and counting!)

They enjoyed being able to manipulate Twitter. To them it was their restaurant, where they got the best table in the house, right by the window. If your opinion was kept off the menu, then it didn't exist.

If you complained, they told you to go build your own restaurant, losers! Then they'd call the Health Department to shut it down. So they needed a velvet rope to protect themselves from you. And now the rope is gone. They are not handling it well. That is why they now think the solution to everything is censorship of ideas and words.

But they no longer call it speech—they call it disinformation, which is now the new "hate speech." If they find your opinion unacceptable in their protected bubble, simply designate it "disinformation" and let the tech titans do the rest. Now just being disagreeable, in public, is a media scarlet letter. They must all be Orwell fans, and for the wrong reasons.

Me? I'm a huge fan of disinformation—because one man's disinformation is another man's information. The solution is to let the ideas play out. If there's anything we learned from the pandemic (which many of us learned before, with climate change, nuclear power, the Iraq War, etc.), the people who claim to own the right information are almost always wrong. I will defend anyone's right to be wrong. Including the Left's. But they won't do the same.

That's quite a flip.

The Flip: Where Did the Flippin' Feminists Go?

Language. Biology. Sports.

If you are a male chauvinist pig right now, you're pretty happy to see what's happening to women within those three areas.

Words have changed, because apparently biology has changed, and sports now must take a backseat to this undoing— a reversal metamorphosis—of biology. The enlightenment is now a deliberate darkening—to replace the objective world of X and Y with they, them, and what the fuck is in your Speedo.

A dude with a penis can be a woman, and not just because his friends say he is because of his new haircut, the color of his shirt, or his love for jazz—it can be depending on how he feels, or if he's going to jail. That's not science. It's actually science fiction. But there's no point discussing it, because everyone agrees it's not science—that war is over. Now it's just gender: it's like giving up on breathing, to focus on your thoughts as you slowly suffocate.

It's like arguing about God to an atheist. Biology is as mockable as the belief in a Creator.

You can't call that progress. Ironically, Richard Dawkins is now the defender of faith—in biology.

But odder still: the people pushing these notions even admit it's no longer traditional feminism, because to them traditional feminism is also too cisnormative (read: bigoted) for the modern activist. If feminism doesn't place trans on the top of the hierarchy of grievance, then frankly you are no different than the dead white males who started all this evil stuff. Well, color me Thomas Jefferson or Weezie Jefferson depending on the mood I'm in. So now men claiming to be women trump biological feminist females.

It feels to me like the modern gender reboot has pretty much rolled back every advancement of the women's movement, with the exception of allowing women to vote. But give it time. A vote might matter more based on how you identify yourself.

Nonbinary could count as two votes.

I might be exaggerating a bit, but some recent developments give me pause. Or rather, menopause.

Since men can now get pregnant, I guess I can finally say it: I have menopause.

I'm in the age group. Sadly, the only hot flashes I get are from Jesse's blow dryer in the makeup chair. He really should only use it to dry the hair on his head, though.

But shit is flowing so fast, so much that it's hard to keep up with the new words, the new antiscience, the changing face of women's sports (which now comes with a five o'clock shadow).

Who knows—maybe in ten years men who identify as women will be able to vote twice, while biological females will make do with one. As a man whose pronoun is now *they*, I might actually count for twelve votes. (I half-joke, mainly because I am short and will likely count as half a vote when we amend the Constitution.) Considering that dead people still vote, it's not as outlandish as it sounds. But short people are discriminated against! The studies show it. So shouldn't I get an extra vote? Why does your identity matter more than mine?

But all that can change depending how they feel. Sometimes *they* feel like a small group; other times *they* can feel like an army.

So here's a question: Why can't I choose to be someone that already exists? And compete with them for their own identity? This isn't a slippery slope, because a slippery slope suggests a wall at the end.

Who knows? Why can't you identify as a specific person? Who owns that identity, at the end of the proverbial, non-biological, nonbinary day? Who really owns a lived experience? If anyone can switch sexes? If consciousness exists independent of the body (which I believe at times, to be true—especially after three edibles), then this body we inhabit contains nothing more than a temporary conduit for my thoughts. So tomorrow I will be Brad Pitt. Even if I look like Greg Gutfeld. I'm totally, literally fluid in the purest sense of fluidity. Sometimes I feel like George Clooney is inside me, and, frankly, it's disappointing when I realize he's not.

It's not about gender identity, it's about identity of all kinds.

I am a six-foot-seven black man currently slumming in a stocky half-Jew loudmouth. If Jill Biden can claim she is a doctor, why can't I identify as Tyrus? *(Because he will beat your ass. —ed.)*

However, with the exception of a few notable voices, the feminists have pretty much retreated to a protective pose—rather than pose tough questions to the new gender militants who've deemed biological sex something replaceable with words. And most notably the most female part of being female can also be male. Aside from Martina Navratilova and J. K. Rowling, where are the women who achieved greatness in a man's world? They're running away from men.

Remember the comedian Sarah Silverman? She used to be a fun comedian with a potty mouth who wore pigtails in her college boyfriend's football jersey well until she was in her forties.

Now she's a middle-aged political activist who earnestly defends trans women's rights (meaning biologically male) as these athletes now compete in the world of female sports. And Silverman believes she knows more than, of all people, the world's greatest trans athlete in history. She dismissed Caitlyn Jenner—who believes that trans females have an advantage over biological females in sports. You know Caitlyn played sports as a man and—unlike Silverman—didn't just wear the jersey.

Silverman actually said, "Caitlyn, you're a woman, right? A trans girl is a girl. She should have the same rights as CIS girls. What, you think a trans girl is too strong? What about tall girls as opposed to short girls? What about the boys in high school who are teeny-tiny and their teammates have already hit puberty and are shaving? Why don't you just have coed sports divided by weight or height, you know? This is so dumb. . . . This is not concern for girls' sports. It's transphobia. Full stop."

Of course, the method she ironically suggests does exist. Boxing, for instance, has weight classes. But if you put a 160-pound female pro boxer in against a 160-pound male pro, he will beat her ass. Every time. That's exactly why we don't mix genders in sports.

But I must admit, when someone says "full stop," it makes me respect the opinion so much more. It's British for saying "period." Why didn't she say "period"? Was it because she knew that trans girls don't have periods? Was she thinking that far ahead?

That's very clever of her . . . or him . . . or they. After all, she is quite fluid. Remember when Sarah reveled in blackface?

Because Comedy Central wouldn't give us approval to use the picture, I commissioned an artist rendering of Sarah Silverman in blackface.

So Sarah slams a trans person. Yes, it's Caitlyn who is hurting trans people by pointing out the obvious transgressions. But Sarah—how arrogant do you have to be to think you know more than Jenner about trans issues and sports? That's like explaining to black people why appearing in blackface makes you a more persuasive authority on civil rights. That seems kinda racist to me . . . full stop!

You aren't the expert . . . on anything. Especially trans rights.

That's like me arguing with Jesse Watters about the effectiveness of hair plugs. He's the expert, not me. Or with Dana Perino about the best way to spay a female dog. By the way, I say take it to a vet. She says do it yourself using ice cubes and a dirt vac.

I bet that Sarah's blackface stunt pretty much killed that endorsement deal she was working on with Maybelline. Yet she's doing okay. Much like you know who. Yes. TV's Jimmy Kimmel, who also reveled in blackface.

Because Comedy Central wouldn't give us approval to use the picture of Jimmy Kimmel in blackface, I did an artist rendering of him in blackface.

What a coincidence. So you see the scam—it's as plain as the shoe polish on someone's blackened face. If you did something now perceived as racist in your past, simply embrace the most woke position, and perhaps you will be spared. It's a retroactive vaccine for assholes, but it means throwing others, like Jenner, under the bus. This is the flip.

We took risks, got caught—and now will tag anyone who dares be the real thing.

No longer are the people living the experience to be respected. So you have Jimmy Kimmel calling Jenner names, but if it were me doing it I would be labeled transphobic (unlike Kimmel's show, Jenner is a regular on my show). Kimmel says, "Is it transphobic to call a trans person an ignorant asshole?"

Of course not, and you're in the clear, Jimmy. You work for Disney. As long as you vote like Goofy, you're good. Of course, if I said that Rachel Levine (once a man, now a lady, and now the assistant secretary for health for the U.S. Department of Health and Human Services) was an ignorant asshole, you'd call me transphobic faster than you can say "Adam's apple."

Credit: AP Images

Silverman, like the rest trying to preserve their careers, realizes that the only way to atone for her blackfaced past is to throw female athletes under the bus. It's why Jimmy, cocreator of *The Man Show*, is now the self-appointed ambassador of wokeness.

Do you remember *The Man Show*? The end credits used to roll over video of girls in bikinis jumping on trampolines. Trust me—I have the tapes. Many, in fact.

Talk about a flip. He went from the most frat-boy bullshit to the mirror image of it. Because, well, he's grown. He's enlightened. *He's terrified.*

Both Silverman and Kimmel share the original sin of blackface and now both employ wokeism as a Kevlar vest to protect themselves from other celebrities. It's prophylactic—an outrage condom.

So the "get out of jail free" card for your unworthy past is to project your past sins on someone else. That is key. Did you know that Silverman and Kimmel dated? I guess the blackface paint rubbed off on each other. It's not a protection racket, it's a protection jacket.

Meanwhile, it's the Right who's calling BS on this.

But also Jenner, who once was a conservative male, but is now a conservative female.

So I guess the intersectionality can only take you so far. Diversity stops at the line called "thought."

Since when did I become a feminist? I usually made fun of that movement, mainly because it was easy, and I was lazy.

True, some of their loudest voices made for wide targets, but I also realize that I was just going after low-hanging fruit. It's the same thing the Left does when they make fun of people who vote Republican—you know, mostly older, white people. Kind of a slow-moving target, wouldn't you say? (You're not wrong.)

Angry people who don't wear makeup or bras are easy to lampoon—but not all of them were like that at all. In fact, many were smart, appealing people—but that was too complicated for a jokester who was in a hurry to write funny stuff.

I have to admit my own ignorance in this. I have to admit this because I have flipped. From nonfeminist to ardent one. I don't own a pussy hat (they don't make one big enough for my head—as my mom complained shortly after childbirth).

Plus I really didn't pay that much attention to feminism—so it was easy thinking that all feminists were the shrieking, proabortion harridans who dressed up as extras from *The Handmaid's Tale* whenever a Supreme Court justice burped.

But now, oddly, I feel for women more than I ever have. And I feel more like a feminist than I think most feminists feel about themselves. I have flipped. No longer Archie Bunker, I've turned into Maude. Yes, an old reference. But the older I get the more I look and sound like Bea Arthur did.

Let's look at the issues.

First, sports.

We watched as male-to-female trans athletes entered sports and creamed the competition like they were Usain Bolt competing in the Special Olympics.

Lia Thomas, once a University of Pennsylvania male swimmer ranked in the 500s nationally, is now a top female swimmer—while towering over the competition like Lurch in the Kentucky Derby locker room. According to press reports (do we know? has anyone asked?), she's keeping her male junk intact. I don't know. But allegedly, that posed a problem not just in the swimming pool, but in the locker room, where everyone changed together. Players complained, but mostly they kept quiet—God forbid you be labeled transphobic, which happened the moment they would raise an objection. What is so alarming is that those who label you transphobic claim such beliefs lead to violence and suicide—so any criticism makes you guilty of murder. Believe me, if that's all it took to off someone, I wouldn't waste that power on trans swimming. There are so many people much more deserving. The cable guy who clogged my toilet, for one.

Thomas easily beat all the biological swimmers, crushing dreams of so many girls who devoted so many years to becoming champions—who now can only settle for second place. How soon before more men become women, and take all the spots?

I doubt many, frankly—because that's a lot of work to win a medal. I mean, you'd have to be mentally ill to do that, right?

But that's not really the issue. In fact, in some sports, introducing trans females could improve it.

The WNBA might actually have dunking. And get some asses in the seats.

Honestly, I'd be one of those asses.

But, again, where are the feminists? (They aren't at WNBA games, that's for sure.)

One feminist, an athlete this time, also felt she knew more than Jenner about this.

Megan Rapinoe, the vocal soccer player who received a medal of honor from President Biden, marginalized any woman who complained—saying there's more to life than sports. It's easy for her to say—she's already made her money off the sport, and she's used to being beaten by men—and boys. A group of teenage boys actually routed her Olympic soccer team for shits and giggles.

Of course, now that she's got her endorsement deals, and celebrity friends and red carpet treatment, she can tell all the young girls in high school getting up at 5 a.m. to practice to basically fuck off. She said, in sum, that if you can't handle trans women beating you in sports, you don't belong.

I could apply that logic to her Olympic achievement if I was as big a creep as she is, by saying your gold medal means shit because you beat women *and not men* for it, so you're really not the best in the world since you believe in this cross-pollination of genders in sports. So shut the fuck up and go shoot another Subway commercial. They have a sandwich named after her called the Rapinoe. It's just a sub roll filled with a pound and a half of bitter greens.

Some feminist. Maybe we should let that high school team play against her in the Olympics next time? Just tell them all to wear dresses.

In fact, as a man, I'm a way better feminist than her. Just like Lea Thomas is a way stronger swimmer than the bio females on her team, I am a better feminist than Rapinoe.

Without even trying. I just have the ability to identify, and that's all it takes.

As a feminist, I believe I can compete easily against those who see biological females as bigoted for noting the obvious biological advantages of a man in women's clothing.

I'm the bravest feminist right now. And I won't stop until I get a medal of freedom. Or an honorary doctorate from Wellesley, or my period . . . whichever comes first.

But again, maybe female soccer could benefit from trans women. Problem is—it's still soccer. Until they can use their hands beyond the sideline throw-ins, what's the point? It wouldn't be interesting unless we gave them sticks to fight it out with. Oh wait, that's hockey.

My favorite story—and one that we covered on *Gutfeld!*—

involved some thirty-year-old guy with a wife and kids. He decided to ditch them, and to identify as female and compete against teenage girls in a street skateboarding championship. And you thought your life was off the rails.

This was a flip, but of the most bizarre kind. It was opportunistic, and selfish, and without much effort done by his part. Sounds like a guy to me!

Grow your hair long, tuck in the junk, and compete against kids. I should have done this in a spelling bee.

He won the five-hundred-dollar prize, crushing "her" competitors—who were thirteen- and fourteen-year-old biological girls! In an interview the trans boarder said without a hint of sarcasm that "she" enjoyed beating the girls, and said there's very little biological difference between them and her twenty-nine-year-old male-bodied self. His statement alone lends credibility to the people who are of the opinion that he/she has to be nuts (no pun intended) to believe this!

If he's kidding, then he's fucking brilliant. He's pulling off a stunt worthy of *Jackass*. But what if he's not? What if he believes this? Then it's mental illness.

But if you call any of this a male mental illness you'll be crucified. But think about it: a guy entering a contest to beat a bunch of girls in skateboarding is a pretty assholish thing to do—and it's something an asshole dude would do!

Except that, well, most men are classy and would rather

open a door for a woman than slam it in her face and say, "I win." (Although, Judge Jeanine always makes the funniest face!)

I feel the same about Leah Thomas—there's something wrong with a person for thinking this is a classy, respectful thing to do. Sure, honey, you're trans . . . but you're also an asshole. A transhole.

Remember when Kimmel called Jenner an asshole? Well, I'll do the same here.

Gutfeld! was the only show to cover the skateboarder—because as I said before, I'm a feminist now. But it was so hilarious, I thought it was a prank. Maybe we'll find out it was. But the boarder walked off with five hundred bucks and some girls didn't. That ain't no prank. And I do wonder how his or her family is doing while she's out chasing her dream of beating young girls in skateboarding. Did his kids get a share of the money? Did it help pay the rent? Or did he buy himself some irregular tits at Marshalls? (Personally, I still think this is a prank. Since then, a bearded male weightlifter entered a contest in Canada to shatter the women's records—while identifying as a woman—and crushing a previous record . . . held by a transwoman.)

For all of this to occur, you need to undermine basic biology.

Which is fine. We've done that already.

The pill made it so you can have sex and not get pregnant.

Same thing with vasectomies.

But both things are rooted in science, specifically biology.

This new attack on women isn't. Let's look at biology. It used to be that you assumed only women can get pregnant. But what if you're a woman who decides to identify as a man! Voilà! Biology is dead! And gender identity takes over. You are no longer a mom, but a pregnant man. And of course, if I decide to identify as a woman, I can do so, with a penis. In fact there are people who now use the phrase "female penis," something I figured was Jesse's nickname in high school. I could go to jail with my junk and live in a women's prison, and fuck up a storm—which one male who identified as female did, knocking up two inmates in New Jersey. Shouldn't two X chromosomes count for something?

Of course, nothing really changes if the uterus is still present, and you still call yourself a dude. It's still a uterus, whether you got a goatee or a snake tattoo on a bicep, or an unrequited love for NASCAR.

Kat Timpf once suggested just saying "people with uteruses versus people not with uteruses"—to replace *male* and *female*. That joke is actually not a joke; it's where we are headed.

But that's a lot of words in Kat's configuration, and call me crazy, but we are more than one of our parts.

That's what my mom used to say.

Sorry, I should have said "birthing person." Because apparently *mom*, *mother*, and *motherhood* are offensive now to *some* people. Who are those people exactly? And can we hit them in the face with mom's rolling pin?

What kind of person thinks the word *mom* is evil? (Not a child, that's *for sure*. But you'll see, this is never about the child's life, but about a delusional adult's.) And what kind of people let that person command respect enough to force companies to actually replace the word in their virtue-signaling emails to all employees? The HR flacks only think about activists and what these activists might do to them—so they gladly insult an entire company instead, or rather the entire history of human civilization—in which moms were almost universally revered. Where are the adults in this conversation?

As a feminist, I support moms, working moms, stay-at-home moms, black moms, white moms, tiger moms, and my favorite moms—the MILFs. As a feminist, since I flipped, I must support all moms, or I am no supporter of women at all.

Because let's not forget—men can't give birth. Women can. And to somehow erase that distinction does no service to females. Instead it gives men another avenue to marginalize biological females. And as a feminist now, I can agree—we've been specializing in that for a long time. And you thought not getting equal pay for doing the same job was sexist? This makes that look like a goddamn Whitman's Sampler.

That's the irony: as women gain more rights in the workplace, activists are removing them from the home. Mom is gone. In comes pregnant dad, along with his new squeeze, a nonbinary birthing person named Destiny. Now British museums are banning the word *mummy* in an effort to not offend dead pharaohs. How this has improved a single life is unclear. No pharaohs could be reached for comment.

Individually, I could not give a shit. Live and let live, I say. But I'm fighting for the words. Because you change the words, you erase facts. Facts about families, facts about biology, and facts about women. It all starts with words. Words are to ideas what fetuses are to babies.

So you see the flip now, don't you?

It's old cranky right-wingers like me who are fighting for the rights of women, while it's so-called feminists who are defending the rights of men who want to be women without even cutting their junk off. Well, except for the feminist contingent that was fighting back against that, and then got called TERFs ("trans-exclusionary radical feminists") so strenuously that they basically retreated, other than J. K. Rowling. That retreat is gutless, actually. Like the guy who waits in the getaway car but left too soon.

What does that tell you? That trans activists are implying that all it takes to be a woman is to say you're a woman. It's gross. Sad, in fact. It's one of things I really love about Caitlyn Jenner, who by the way didn't transition until she headed into her seventh decade. Talk about patience. I dig that completely. She waited until all the kids had grown and had their own kids! That's conservatism with a twist.

But she made it clear she didn't have the history that women

Mom, Chipper, and me—
home from school. Chipper
never liked me. Can't say I
blamed him.

Gramps, Greg, and Les.
Naked-lady statue kept far away
from Gramps.

Dad and me before sister
Chris's wedding.
Yes, that's shag carpet.

My first lesson in cars—
if you know nothing about
them, don't buy a
Facel Vega.

My fortieth birthday in Ibiza. My eyes tell you everything.

Me and Jackie hanging out in Belmont, CA. Where I got most of my talent.

Elena and me at New York City Hall, waiting to get married. I make no apologies for those lapels.

In Greece at a wedding. I have no idea what I did to make her happy.

In Tulum, Mexico, Elena can't find her pants.

Sister and wife in good spirits before I get obnoxious and ruin everything.

Elena enjoying an airport lounge before I recognized her.

Me and sis heading to the White House. Clearly, we were very excited or on amphetamines.

Wife deliriously happy that I am away, traveling.

Manager and lifelong friend Aric Webb with Elena at some bar in Soho. He helps her put up with me.

Riley and his awesome pop, Brendan Gale, first meeting at a bar
in Texas—we instantly became friends; RIP, Riley.

I met the legendary Brenda Lee backstage in Nashville.
I love her, and not just cuz I found someone shorter than me.

Meeting of the outsiders at Sunset Marquis.
With novelist Walter Kirn; King Buzzo of Melvins; pop genius Ariel Pink; Vandals founder, Joe Escalante, and his wife, Sandra; musician Jon David; and manager, Aric Webb.

Took a train with Norm McDonald to his show and hung with him the whole night. A great comedian and a brilliant human, RIP.

A Misfits sandwich, with Jerry Only and Glen Danzig, backstage at Newark's reunion concert.

Kid Rock and me at Rob O'Neill's wedding. We all did shots to the face in Rob's honor.

A piece of art from the legendary hot rod artist the Newtonator, Ed Newton.

This is what Dana wears to work.

At Hershey Park, Dana and me nervously waiting to see how many rides we aren't going to enjoy.

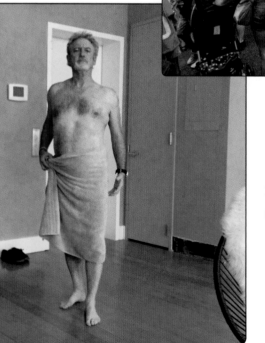

Larry Gatlin shows up at my place regularly to use my shower.

Kinda shocking: running into myself at the subway. Even more shocking: it's not defaced (yet).

John Rich, Larry Gatlin, and Oprah.

One of the legendary Saturday shows, with great actor Dan Roebuck and Jordan Peterson.

Kat's hair extensions cooling off after a long day.

The only show to feature intergalactic monsters (Gwar) and earthly disasters (Jesse Watters).

Tyrus giving me the look.

Arriving at Nashville. Literally and figuratively.

Meat Loaf and Robert Johnson after our live show in Nashville.
RIP, Meat—a monstrously great man.

Judge Jeanine talks tough to my sister, Leslie, and malcontent cohost.

Guess who this is.
Hint: She talks fast and
will cheer at my funeral.
(Second hint: initials are E.C.)

Tom Shillue and Walter Kirn
at my lake house. Tom draws
and Walter reads while I hide
in the bushes.

Tom Shillue in all his Shillue glory
after taking a dip in the lake at my
cabin. Admit it: he's gorgeous.

The person behind the person: my amazing assistant, Elle Penner, who would not exist without me (I introduced her parents to each other).

The Gutfeld staff (plus friends, neighbors, and a member of the Misfits) at my fifty-eighth birthday.

Before fame:
Gus trying his best
to be adorable
(and succeeding).

After fame:
Gus starring in his
first Super Bowl ad
(King of Late Night spot).

Gus, after hours of
constipation, poops
a rope.

Russell Brand and I hug and made up.

had—no pregnancies and no periods and of course no crush on Bruce Jenner. Full stop! Well, maybe she does have a crush on Bruce Jenner. Could you blame her?

Of course, there's more to being female than biology.

But there's a difference between men and women, the kind of difference that should make for celebration, not erasure. And of course, you can do what you like in America. So if you're an adult who realizes you're in the wrong gender, do what you need to do. (Actually, by that logic, can I identify as a middle-aged male whose loans are fully paid off? Wait, why not? Millions of college kids are doing it.)

We just can't do it at the expense of other people, or confused kids. Seriously, if a child came to his parents and said, "I don't feel like a boy," and the right-winger said, "Cool, let's chop it off and make you a girl so you don't grow up to be gay," the Left would go insane. It's conversion therapy with a knife. But it's not the Right behind this. It's the radical Left.

It's the worst kind of flip: deciding that surgery is preferable to letting a child grow into the person they want to be—gay or straight. Why the rush, woke lefties? Are you miserable in your own skin and just want company as soon as possible?

Think about it: the most insidious flip you're seeing is from the Left, in their abandonment of gays and lesbians. If my male relative, who is gay, had expressed an affinity for boys when he was eleven, perhaps the old right would have put him through conversion therapy to switch his orientation. That's now considered evil. But here we have people saying, "No, this is better: let's just cut off his dick and make him a woman." After all, he's simply *penis-centric*—the worst kind of patriarchy.

The flip means a deliberate death of a gay person, turning him into a her. It's killing off a person to create a new one. And it's not based in science, but in a delusion. The vast majority of kids who "express" this sort of dysmorphia will ultimately grow up to be gay or lesbian, if we allow it to play out (docs used to call this "do no harm"). But forcing the issue early obviously reduces the population of adult gays and lesbians. If Republicans were behind this, then the Left would scream. It's also strange to even consider "blocking" puberty. It's only something every human must go through. And it sucks *for everyone.* Putting it off is no substitute for getting it over with.

Flipping a Men's Magazine into an Anti-Men's Magazine with the Help of Little People

Running *Stuff* magazine was one of the best experiences of my life. I put it right up there with taking peyote and then sitting in my car as it went through a car wash.

I took a magazine with a circulation of 700,000 and more than doubled it in a year—and created more controversy than any editor currently alive, and did it without trying. I did it by pointing out absurdity in the medium itself.

The controversies I created were all centered on teasing—or, in modern vernacular, trolling. I trolled everyone from editors at the *New York Times* to editors of *GQ* and *Esquire* and even my sister publication, *Maxim.* My trolling was relentless. I started a comic strip that lampooned the publishing industry (featuring known pompous players in the scene and exposing their incompetence and elitism), and it got picked up everywhere from the *Times* to *USA Today*—because I knew that people in media loved nothing more than stories about the media. Even if what they picked up was making fun of them specifically (half the time they were too clueless to notice).

After lampooning Art Cooper, then editor of *GQ*, he wrote to the owner of the company that published *Stuff,* Felix Dennis, demanding that he fire me.

Felix immediately shared the letter with me, laughing hysterically as he read it out loud. The letter was serious, angry, and full of the typical arrogance you'd get from a pompous ass who thinks with the snap of a finger he could fire someone who pisses them off. Maybe it worked with waiters. But not here.

Felix demanded I do something with it. When I heard that, I think I tore muscles in my face, my grin was so wide.

When I got hold of the letter, I sent it to a handwriting expert to analyze Cooper's personality. The expert produced a detailed analysis, describing the writer as deeply insecure and vain.

Then I took the results and shared them with the New York tabloids. It went everywhere, but the *Daily News* printed it all.

Shortly after, Cooper ended up losing his job. Then, sadly, shortly after (like weeks), he passed away from a stroke in a restaurant. The two events are not connected, thankfully. But some idiots still blame me for it. Like I'm the one who set the market price for lobster at that restaurant on that fateful day.

But, come on, I had never expected anyone to write a letter to my boss to have me fired, and Cooper probably never expected that I would turn that letter into fodder for comedy. No one thought he'd die from a stroke at a prominent table at a tony Manhattan restaurant, oddly having a meal in a room with the very editor who had replaced me at *Men's Health*. There's a parable in there somewhere, but thankfully I don't know what a parable is.

Boredom with conventional activities brings strokes of genius and also trouble.

Sometimes it ends up being harmless and strange. Like, for example, when I was asked to sit in the front row at a big fashion show and I didn't want to go. Then I looked down at the floor of our lobby, and saw a bearskin rug, complete with head.

Then I knew what I would do. I went to the fashion show, wearing the full bearskin.

And little else. I still do this at Fox sometimes. Brit Hume loves it.

It was an interesting scene: What do you do, as a fashionista, when you come across something like me? Do you take in the surreal monstrosity with good humor, or think, quite correctly, that I'm taking the piss out of you, the pretentious fashionista?

The crowd was split down the middle, people seated near me were terrified, although the late fashion legend André Leon Talley begged me for a picture, which ended up in one of his famous dispatches.

That was a stunt, a harmless one. But they do add up. And when you pile on the mayhem, your bosses start to think that maybe you fashion yourself bigger than the company you work for (they were right).

If you keep doing it, well, you'll certainly pay for it at some point.

When an association of magazine publishers asked me to

speak at a conference featuring industry insiders about how to create media buzz, I initially turned it down. Why do I need to tell these idiots my secret, I thought? If they need a conference on how to attract attention, then they're beyond hopeless. Tell them to hit the road.

But then, in my itching boredom, I saw an opportunity: if they want someone to teach them how to create buzz, maybe I'm the right person to do it, without actually being there at all! At a bar, I came up with a way to do just that.

At a local Mexican joint, I called my friend Jeffrey Beacher, who had run a comedy show called *Beacher's Madhouse*, and asked him if he knew any "little people." His casual response: "How many do you need?" I bought tickets to the conference and gave them to three little people—one dressed as a gangster, another as a businessman, and another in a top hat and a cane—who would show up and ask questions that would disrupt the meeting. I would not be present at this conference. Bill Schulz, then a features editor for *Stuff*, was there to make sure it went off without a hitch. And it did go off—but with a *lot* of hitches. Putting Bill Schulz in charge of something to make sure things run smoothly is like putting . . . oh, I don't know: something like making Jerry Sandusky a crossing guard at an all-boys Catholic elementary school. (I kid. Bill actually did a great job controlling the unfolding chaos.)

When the symposium began, it seemed pretty calm and

dull, like your typical conference. But then the little guys started to pepper the panelists with inane questions. They asked the editor of *O: The Oprah Magazine,* who the magazine was named after; they asked the editor of *Rolling Stone* why their magazine sucked. They took phone calls and aggressively chomped on potato chips. They talked loudly and incessantly—daring the audience and the hosts to call them out—but everyone was too scared of offending the little folks. Little people can get away with a lot. Trust me, I know.

Finally a brave woman in the audience stood up and said, "Can't we see that something is going on here?" But everyone was still too petrified to say anything.

Because, you know, it was little people, and no one wanted to point out the obvious: that it's very rare that there is *one* little-person journalist at a conference, let alone *three*—but the audience had to pretend it was normal.

The other panelist on the dais, the editor in chief of *Maxim,* looked on in confusion, and he started to get angry, since everyone assumed he was behind the chaos. After all, who else would do this but some knucklehead from *Maxim*? He vehemently denied it. When I heard about this, I was deeply offended: there was no way anyone from *Maxim* would be clever enough to come up with this.

Then perhaps it dawned on the Maxim flack that it was me. And so, someone called the bosses.

Finally, moderator Cindi Leive demanded that the little guys leave, which is when the leader of the bunch said, "Is it because I'm short?"

She retorted: "No—I'm short, too!"

Meanwhile, I was at the Sunset Marquis in West Hollywood sitting in a bathrobe, drinking by the pool, ready to interview Pamela Anderson about her new movie. At least she *said* she was Pamela Anderson. (It might have been Louie Anderson.) The prank made all the papers—creating my future firing—while I was having dinner with Lux Interior and Poison Ivy of the Cramps at their house overlooking a California cemetery.

I was fired a week or so later.

Well, actually not fired. I was brought in to see the CEO, Stephen Colvin. He was a very sweet and engaging guy, but was angry at me lately. This time it was for being taken by surprise. "Why didn't you tell me you were doing this?" he asked. "Because you would have said no," I said. He replied, "You're right." He sat silently, and then told me that I would no longer be editor of the magazine.

At least he didn't make me "editor at large."

He added that an editor I had fired months earlier after he dared me to fire him (never, ever do that, trust me—for obvious reasons) would be taking my place.

This editor, also a very nice guy, has the distinction of being the first person I ever fired in my career. But I only did it because he dared me. I never would have done it in the first place—but when someone throws down a gauntlet like that, you have to accept it.

I genuinely liked John, but you just can't dare people to fire you, assuming they won't.

And by "people" I mean me.

When Colvin fired me, he redefined it as yet another job transition.

He said that I would become the "director of brand development" for Dennis Publishing, to be situated somewhere in Los Angeles, far away from the products that I had obviously contaminated. That was the goal: get Greg away from the product ASAP.

I said, "Okay, sure, whatever." But then I thought for a bit and asked Steve, "You are putting me in charge of brand development—are you telling me this is a promotion?" (I knew that it wasn't.) He saw an opening to placate me and said, "Yes, it's a promotion." I said, "Cool. Then, if it's a promotion, I would get a raise then right? I want fifty grand more than my salary." He looked at me, calculating the damage he might avoid if he just agreed. So he did. I also got a fully paid-for apartment in LA (in the gloomy Oakwood complex near the Galleria) and a rental car—a convertible Chrysler Sebring that screamed "divorced dad with porn obsession."

So, for a year I skulked around Hollywood, taking meetings, producing a play, dating Scientologists, and knocking out one or two shows for MTV, while drinking and doing drugs and figuring out the rest of my life. *Stuff* magazine ended up heading into fast decline, and then folded for lack of energy and creativity. It needed more little people, literally and figuratively.

As my year in career limbo started to peter out, out of the blue I got a call from England, from Dennis Publishing again, the crew who just told me my year was about to be up in Los Angeles.

The fact is, they loved my work but couldn't handle my weirdness. That is likely my epitaph. I'm guessing they felt the same way about me that the Rolling Stones did with Brian Jones. (Note to Gen Z: the Rolling Stones are a British rock band, which Jones was a member of until they killed him.)

But what I had done for *Stuff* was now gonna happen for *Maxim UK*. They wanted danger, surprise, and stunts. And I was their guy. So the mad genius Felix Dennis, who had fired me once already, decided to rehire me. Of course when he rehired me he said, quite frankly, "This is going against my instincts." (If I had a nickel for every time I've heard that right before a woman said yes to a date . . .)

I realized he had to be convinced to hand over the reins to

me once again. The problem with Felix was that we were too much alike, and he knew that. He was as reckless and offensive as I was—the only difference was that he got rich selling his computer mags. He was me—but with a Bentley and a whorehouse. (This is true. Felix had a bordello in London. I never got to go, but I heard good things, usually standing outside a window.)

I went to London and helmed the wildest iteration of a magazine to exist in modern times. I knew that this kind of men's magazine was dying faster than a Kennedy with a pilot's license. I mean, who needed a men's mag with half-naked women and shiny cars—when the internet offered that and more? So I realized that my goal in the next two years was to create a joyful kamikaze publication that undermined all the conventions of mainstream magazines. I decided that I would flip the script entirely—turn a beer-and-babes trash mag into a homoerotic, surreal attack on a media's version of male culture.

And boy did we. There were things in *Maxim UK* that no one would ever see again. I hired a talented editor from the *Pink Paper*, a gay rag, to write my sex features. I came up with a comic strip called *Gooligans*, which followed the antics of violent gay hooligans. The goal was to show what would happen if gay men were no different than straight men, which isn't the case—no matter what your female gender teacher with muttonchops like Quint from *Jaws* tells you. Well, some parts are the same.

This is Gooligans—an attempt to envision gay men with straight flaws.

I created *DogBaby*, a gruesome comic strip based on a fatuous *GQ* article that told men that the way to pick up women is to either take kids to the park or get a dog (being able to care for dogs and babies means you're a stable person who can be a good dad in the future). The strip involved a lonely acne-scarred male who in his basement conjoins a dog and a baby to take to the park or a mall to pick up women.

Credit: MaximUK/June 2005

"Dogbaby"—a comic strip likely never to be replicated again.

This monstrosity, DogBaby, was constantly writhing in pain from this insane experiment in species fusion. But true to the advice of *GQ*, it helped its owner pick up chicks. The owner (his likeness was based on one of my good-looking art directors who commissioned the work) would head to some public place where young women frequent, and the sickly DogBaby would attract females who became smitten with the selflessness of the owner, the saint who took care of the monster mutt. And as always in the final panel, the guy would leave the dog behind to get laid nearby in the bushes. We would show them fucking, as the dog suffered in isolation. It was a sick and strange idea, but within it was something truthful. Please let me know what that it is because I still am not sure.

There were also features we did that would never get past the bosses now.

Because what I asked of my writers would have been considered sexual harassment.

Two examples:

The sex doll holiday. One afternoon I ordered a sex doll that cost roughly eight thousand dollars. It was malleable, human-size, and weighed maybe 120 pounds. It was brunette, with three functioning orifices for lonely perverts. It had a dead face, which perhaps also lent further appeal for lonely freaks.

When it arrived, I assigned a very talented young writer named Martin Robinson the mission to spend a romantic weekend with the doll—check into a posh hotel, take the doll to nice restaurants (that required reservations), and other touristlike endeavors (I remember a gondola ride being especially creepy).

The feature had a premise: men were in decline, in terms of romantic pursuers. No one dated in London, as far as I could tell—and most men were finding their sexual release in porn. I figured that this somehow would be one next step. We did this story maybe twenty years ago. It has proved very prescient, and grimly so.

I never questioned Martin about whether or not he did sleep with the doll, but I realize that it's a story you could likely never do again. I am still not sure what happened to that doll.

I just hope it was taken to a car wash. At least it couldn't complain to HR. Last I heard it's in the running to be a host for *The Daily Show*.

Another story that would get me fired today is when I assigned one of my staff writers to become a "full monty" stripper for a male review in Brighton, England. "Nick" gamely did so, and, along with other male coworkers, stripped to nothing in front of a large crowd, which included my wife and, well, other staffers and their partners. I can't imagine ever doing that again. I also won't forget one of my other heavy-drinking writers, coming along for the ride to the beachfront town, where he proceeded to sleepwalk minus his own clothes. He wasn't even hired to do that! He did it for free! Anyway, *he* should be the host of *The Daily Show*.

One night I woke up with that same writer standing in our room in a naked haze. Then he walked downstairs, and went to sleep on a lobby couch of the hotel, buck naked. Thankfully, a couple staying at the resort got him towels and a blanket. One of the curses of having him stay over at your place: he never stays in one spot. A year or so before that, I found him urinating in my kitchen, again while sleepwalking. I hadn't even known he was in town!

The *Maxim* experiment ran its course in two years. It experienced quick success and then it flatlined, like all those mags did. And, to his defense, Felix got tired of calling me into his office to tell me I was evil (which he did, in the most affectionate way). It was really hard to be yelled at by your boss when behind his desk where he sat and chain-smoked these awful British cigarettes there was a painting of him naked.

Felix made me allergic to Bentleys, because when his driver would park his massive luxury sedan in front of the office to take me to see Felix at his house, I knew I was about to be fucked, and not in a good way. Rather, in a British boarding school, Dickensian, Victorian steampunk sort of way.

As beautiful as the car was, it became for me a moving casket, all leather and sleek brass, complete with crystal tumblers and mysterious buttons that controlled God knows what. But once I got in, it turned into a hearse, the driver silently driving me to my own funeral.

I would sit there, in Felix's waiting outer chamber—dying to pee, because that's what happens when you know you're going to get filleted in a foreign country. Felix was tired of me—but for things that he found hilarious in private. He was a hypocrite in that regard.

An infamous article called "The Ikea Sex Party" was perhaps the final straw, or Allen wrench.

An idea created and written by the great Michael Dent pitched to me while he was at the *Pink Paper*, it took Ikea instructions to the next level, turning them into a sex manual so you could have sex while you put the dresser or bed together.

Felix found it hilarious. He literally was choking with laughter when he was reading to me over the phone one afternoon.

But then Ikea called and threatened to sue. In a stupid Swedish accent, I'm guessing.

In response to the suit, an editor for the Prague edition of *Maxim* decided to run my story out of joyful spite, which only made it worse. The Ikea sex party lives in infamy . . . but good luck finding it anywhere. They buried it like Jimmy Hoffa, never to be seen again. It became yet another nail in my coffin as editor—a coffin you could construct while also having sex.

Up until his death (obviously not beyond that), Felix would bring it up to me and tell me how horrible it was. I had to remind him that he told me it was the best thing he'd ever seen. He would say, "Maybe so, Greg, but it was poor judgment." He was likely right. We were close friends after the firing, and he even did my show *Red Eye* a couple of times, to remind me what trouble I was. One of the last things he said to me on TV was, "When I fired you the third time, I made sure you stayed fired." That wasn't hard, considering the magazine folded shortly thereafter. (Before he died, Felix wrote collections of poetry that actually rhymed. They were brilliant. To quote Don Lemon, "Google it.")

The Age Flip

You sensed the trend. Today, most news outlets are just high-tech versions of supermarket tabloids, the ones with headlines like "Amazing Rooster Cries Tears That Look Like Jesus," and "Pop Rocks That Cure Cancer." But now it incorporates political adversaries and issues.

But all the weirdest, wrongest stories went in one direction. There would be a fake story about Trump watching a hooker pee on another hooker in a Russian hotel room. But there would never be a fake story about Hunter watching a hooker pee on another hooker in a hotel room . . . even though we now know, for Hunter, that's called Tuesday.

But a weird thing happened since Trump: all the young comedians decided that it was more important to be solemn and outraged than outrageous and funny. And in a refreshing fashion, it was the vets, the older dudes, who were taking the risks, and defying the mob. The OGs have really stepped up.

You see this split in comedy, largely because some comedians truly fear for their fledgling careers—while others who've made it can actually say "fuck you" to the mob. The young ones think that they won't make it unless they embrace the new way of thinking, but because the new way is not funny, they have much less chance of making a name for themselves taking that route.

This could explain why the younger comics mimic the woke, while the Dave Chappelles and the Ricky Gervaises don't.

The old are the new young. The young are the new old. I think I feel a song coming on.

Cancel culture has created a Benjamin Button effect in that older generations start behaving the way their kids should. And I don't mean "acting young," as in getting piercings and taking up skateboarding in board shorts—I mean real honest renegade thinking, and saying things that are risky today.

We've confused what connotates risk. It's not saying "America's hopelessly racist," when it's the status quo legacy media saying that every day.

It's not saying that capitalism sucks, when even capitalists now pretend to be socialists just to keep the teens buying their slave-labor-produced shoes and phones.

I'm talking about saying things that go against that prevailing wisdom of the media. We see that the only reason for liberals to embrace this stuff is to stay safe—if it maintains your popularity, if it gets you good grades in school, and allows you to climb the corporate ladder faster, then just put your head down and say yes.

In comedy, the risk-takers are the ones battling the safe spacers—from John Cleese to Gervais. I'd throw in Nick Di Paolo (who, I should note, writes for my show), Andrew Schulz, Tim Dillon, David Spade, Colin Quinn, Dennis Miller, Joe Rogan (and lots of his comedian guests), Chappelle, Russell Brand, Rob Schneider, and Jim Breuer. Outside of comedy, I would include J. K. Rowling, Morrissey, King Buzzo, Eric Clapton, Johnny Rotten, and Van Morrison.

Most of these are boomers and aging Gen Xers who take real risk against wokeism. It may be because they've been through it before—they recognize it. Many of these folks "fought the man" in the 1960s and 1970s. Now there's a new "man." But it identifies as something else.

Of course, the risks are easier when you've got seven or nine figures in the bank accounts.

But not all of them are rich. Some are far from it. They're just natural rebels.

That should be an incentive for everyone else to do the same. So these old farts are standing up to the mob, who are chasing them not with pitchforks but smartphones.

Chappelle especially. Last summer a Minneapolis club called First Avenue canceled one of his shows because of a few online complaints from people who labeled the comedian transphobic, based on bits from his previous shows. I've seen his shows—and surprise, I disagree on their transphobic claim. But that's not the point. The point is that when faced with maybe fifty to a hundred signatures on an online post, the club caved. They could be defined by one word: *pussies*.

But Chappelle didn't cave. He has so far not complied to the faceless mob (and neither did Netflix, to their credit). Instead he becomes even more determined to do his job honestly. Like someone half his age, he's giving the finger to the man, who oddly might be a group of people half his age. Which makes my head hurt. I let my staff do the math, and they're off today picking up my laundry and vacuuming food crumbs from Jesse's toupee tree.

So, the flip is obvious: the old guy is now the daredevil and the young ones are delicate daffodils who claim they must be protected from jokes. And they compel you to comply.

The young are now so pathetic that they could not even simply skip the damn show (which is what normal people would do; just stay home and whack off to Hannah Gadsby, if that's possible). Even if they did go to the show, and didn't like a joke, they could simply leave. But instead they take the coward's way out and write a petition. Throw a public tantrum, then pluck a pronoun for their Twitter bio. They're only strong in large groups in anonymous forums.

But one thing is for sure: they got the club to give in to their absurd demands. And it got Chappelle booted to another, better club! And got him priceless publicity. I'm wondering now if he didn't write the petition himself, actually. Maybe I need to try this on my book tour.

First Avenue's explanation was that although they believe in diverse voices, and the freedom of artistic expression, blah blah blah. *Fuck you.*

Think about that for a minute. If artistic expression didn't have an impact, then defending its right to exist wouldn't be necessary. What would be the point of defending safe artistic expression?

Next time book Patton Oswalt. Not only would his artistic output not need defending, but you'd never have any risk for unrest since the audience would be fast asleep. Or nonexistent, more likely.

So while the young prefer security, the old are out taking risks. I'm fifty-eight . . . does that make me old? It makes me older than a lot of people, but also younger, too.

Am I taking more risks than I did when I was younger?

In many ways, no. For example, I drank recklessly when I was young. I worked out relentlessly. I was always chasing a party. I was actively trying to shut off my brain through destructive activity. I sometimes wonder, if the Greg of now met the Greg of old, would he like him? Maybe as a drinking buddy.

The Greg of the past was as sick and strange and out of control as you see on TV.

So we might get along. But my advice would be to stop trying to escape your thoughts. Embrace them, no matter how subversive they are.

My humor was always subversive (or as the press describe it, "quirky"). But it started to gain a critical antipathy when my politics were exposed.

Before, when I edited *Men's Health*, then *Stuff*, then *Maxim UK*, people could find my strange sense of humor confusing or endearing—but rarely political.

I would say that now I'm still apolitical, unless I have to address a political topic. And of course, that's now every single day of my career on *The Five*. I am forced to, and I enjoy most of it. But if it wasn't for *The Five*, I honestly don't know if I would think at all about political races or scandals. I would live a life likely detached from all of it. Except crime and taxes and drugs. Because those are things that directly affect my life.

So now, old Greg takes many more risks than young Greg. Every day I speak to millions of people, and say things off the top of my head (but prepared, oddly) that engender the wrath of cancel culture. I know this because they clip my comments daily and then feed them to media outlets every single day. I'm creating more jobs for media shut-ins than the current administration.

The anti-Fox bloggers are an industry in itself—a pathetic one, to boot. And so low-risk.

Imagine having the job of watching *The Five*, and waiting for me or Jesse to say a joke, and then to clip it. It's no different than getting paid to sit in a bar and eavesdrop on people who are having a better time than you.

The people who have that job, whether it's at Media Matters or the Daily Beast, are likely half my age (God, if they're not, and older, then they truly are pathetic and needed a better therapist). So they are young people who, from the safety of their cubicle or studio apartment (in New York, the two are indistinguishable), are trying to call out people who are walking tightropes of intense conversation every day. Professional hall monitors. Narcs.

This is the opposite of how you should spend your youth.

You should never become a media cop as your sole career, auditing shows on TV. It's literally the opposite of living your own life! It's living someone else's life, and then providing bitter, but not better, CliffsNotes.

Meanwhile, the people living their lives, like me, take risks every day. And love it.

Because, every time I open my mouth, I'm cliff diving.

It's a risk. To talk about crime, immigration. Gender. Race.

But it's not a risk to listen and then audit it for an audience that hopefully clicks on your post. That's the opposite of risk.

It's the ultimate cowardice, essentially hiding in the back, hoping you're not chosen next for the firing squad.

There is no way I could do what they do. (A young Greg wouldn't.)

It really should be the opposite. Young people take the risks, and old farts like me criticize it from our well-manicured lawns. "Stop speeding, you idiots!"

But now it's young writers who seek to punish people for speaking opinions that they find offensive (except, of course, they really don't find these opinions offensive at all—it's simply filling a hole, where one's own achievement should be, it's a performance, not an opinion.).

I could never do this. When I was young, when I needed a job because I was broke and wanted a career, I moved to Allentown, Pennsylvania, and worked for a health magazine called *Prevention.* I wrote health articles for old people. I interviewed doctors. I went to medical conferences. It was fun, hard work. It doesn't sound exciting at all: to be explaining estrogen replacement therapy to middle-aged moms. (Which might explain the late-night websites I frequent.) But the work had to be careful. If you screwed up, you could hurt someone. So I did my research and wrote each article as if it was intended for my mom. To make sure of that, I had a picture of my mom next to my computer. So when I had an issue trying to explain some new drug or therapy, I would look at that picture, and attempt to explain it to *her*. It worked. (The writing trick, not the therapy. I still have the itchy rash.)

My mother, by the way, was a risk-taker—much in the way I am now. She said what was on her mind, no matter how outrageous. If a TV producer had run into her in the 1970s onward, they would have pointed a camera at her and started rolling.

I did pretty much that. A risk I took at *Stuff* magazine was transcribing the messages my mom would leave on my answering machine. Then I created a column called "Ask Greg's Mom," where she'd answer relationships and life lesson questions from readers. Then at *Red Eye*, I would do a segment with her, sometimes nightly, to review the previous night's show. It was a calamity—you never knew if she would answer the door during the segment, if someone came knocking, or she would hang up in midsentence, or yell at me for being rude to a guest.

She was in her eighties at the time, and she didn't give a damn.

Maybe that's part of the flip, too.

The older you get, the less time you have to care about what other people think.

But, in defense of the young, they have more to lose at life's casino, in terms of years. Getting canceled at twenty-five is far worse than fifty-five or sixty-five. Maybe that explains the death of risk and rise of this tattletale mentality. In fact, that could be the answer *for all of this*.

For one, you're likely broke (unless you have rich parents), and once you're canceled no one's going to touch you for years thanks to the immortality of infractions within social media. Make a joke about Black Lives Matter—then see how your career goes. You'll be sweeping out train stations for the next forty years.

But I would ask the young: don't forget that old people were once young, too.

They have seen a lot. And hopefully, they've accrued wisdom along the way. Or at least, some debts. Which are a source of wisdom, believe me. Combine that with wealth and diminished time ahead. They then ask themselves, why should I be afraid of the mob? Meanwhile, the young see their cries for safe spaces to be a sign of rebellion!

Do you remember those white BLM protesters surrounding a woman at brunch demanding she raise her fist?

That is about as conformist and risk-free as it gets. Especially when there are a hundred of them.

They embrace the opposite of risk, which is "might makes right."

So in this flip, why do the young decide that being an individual is less attractive than joining a faceless horde? We used to embrace the rebel who stood out, from James Dean onward. The closest thing we have to James Dean now is Ben Shapiro or maybe Ryan Long. I would have said me, but let's face it, I've been aged out. I'm James Dean with a "do not resuscitate" bracelet.

They have their reasons, but their reasons are ones that

we've all faced and rejected throughout our lives. We could have bent to the mob, but we didn't.

True, maybe Gen Zers are scared of the mob turning on them. Or perhaps they're doing what they think is popular (something we've all been tempted with growing up—even I got a perm once). Or maybe they've fallen in love with the attention they get for being aggrieved (it's a good feeling—you get sympathy and admiration from your fellow losers).

Or maybe they suck.

In the old days before the flip, we used to say "Those who can't do, will teach." Now it's "Those who can't do, will try to cancel those who can." Envy drives cancel culture, like it drives every destructive behavior. If you can't have what others have, or do what others do, then burn it all down. Then they make these demands publicly in groups, like the Chappelle petition. They never do it one-on-one. It's always in packs because there's safety in numbers—even if all those numbers are zeros.

The Five Flips the Script

Yeah—you get it. I am a risk. But as I got older and wiser, I decided to play a longer game. And after I got more daily exposure, I found an audience who embraced my weirdness, because it was balanced with a moral wisdom that I also possessed, but rarely showed.

It appeared in *Red Eye*, but really took hold at *The Five*.

This is a strange thing: Why is it that a personality fit for 3 a.m. gets only more popular at 5 p.m., when families are just preparing for dinner? Shouldn't I fail miserably, after deeply offending millions of people? That's what the critics hoped. But, nope. The most offensive person on earth became America's teddy bear (with head lice).

The Five was a gamble. Glenn Beck had just gone, and he was a big deal at Fox. That left an open spot at 5 p.m. The late Roger Ailes had this idea about a show called *The Five* and threw some anchors together to give it a shot as a summer replacement. In my initial meeting a producer told me that my role would be limited—as comic foil for one block, I'd do a monologue and shoot it around for questions. That was it. I would basically take a backseat for the rest of the segments. Sure, sounds good to me.

Problem was, during the rehearsals, the best parts of the show were of me and some broad named Dana Perino trading insults, teasing each other like classmates with an unexpected affinity for each other. Who would have guessed two people with a combined height of Bill O'Reilly would see eye to eye on a lot of things?

The people in charge realized they had a hit on their hands, before it even aired. I was told, "You and Dana are set, so is [Bob] Beckel—we'll figure out the rest."

The show premiered in 2011. The typical reviews from the

typical types predicted a quick death. It would last weeks, perhaps a few months at most. Now here in 2023, as I write this, I can tell you the show ended up rated number one in *all* of television. There we were, at 5 p.m., slaughtering prime time on every network. The thing was a fucking juggernaut. I don't think any of us saw this coming, but when we look back at it, it makes total sense.

With that *Five* success, no one sat us down and told us what to do.

The structure was simple. *The Five* is at 5 p.m. with five hosts, and there are basically five segments (not counting "One More Thing," which was Dana's brilliant idea). The first segment would be the A block, which is the biggest story, where a host would read a script off the teleprompter and the rest of us would comment on it. It was that simple.

Other people tried to copy this formula, but they failed hilariously because they were missing key elements. *Us.*

It wasn't like anything on television—except maybe *Red Eye*—only because *Red Eye* was also a panel, featuring me. (I ended up leaving *Red Eye* after helming both shows for a few years. My schedule, and my liver, couldn't take it.) *The Five* was more commercial, sleeker and professional. People tuned in, but not just to hear about politics, but to see how Dana might react to my obnoxious comments, or how Beckel, who may or may not have been up all night gambling on horses or women, might react to anything that upset him.

The Five could have been like any talk show, except that it was surprising and funny—and reflected exactly what you would remember best from a dinner with friends and relatives.

Plus, we gave something to the Right that they really needed: *friends.*

Constantly told by the media that they were unlikable, close-minded jerks, here was a show that flipped the script entirely. We were now the cool people having fun. This is why *Red Eye* was so important—it showed that conservatives could be fun, and like different music, and joke around, and embrace while mocking pop culture. It gave people a way to feel like you weren't just going to be a boring bow tie if you embraced this political mindset. We could and would talk about anything; we took more risks, we told more jokes. By comparison, the staid liberal shows took on the veneer of yesterday's news.

If you looked at our show, you saw we were usually laughing. If you looked at other shows, they were shrieking, grimacing. Thanks to Trump, Joe Scarborough from *Morning Joe* morphed into a Karen in drag, demanding a new person be arrested every episode, while his wife nodded along because that's what they pay her for. Or maybe it was the other way around. Who knows. I can't really tell the two apart.

The time slot for *The Five* should have been a challenge. It wasn't. How can you get eyeballs when everyone is getting off work, anyway? Well, it did. People made sure they were home to watch it. Word of mouth became the best promotion. I compare it to a real life version of *Friends*, which would be a brilliant insight had I ever watched that show. But you didn't need actors playing people who pretended to get along—you had real people actually getting along. Without scripts and at a fraction of the cost, we were doing this every day, and it was—with brief exceptions—an unmitigated joy.

I had a dream job. As someone who was a class clown, I was now being paid to be the class clown. I was not being a comedian (I was never that), but I operated as an alert host who was there to keep things light and unpredictable—to pierce through the shrieking solemnity of political commentary; to remind ourselves that we should never take ourselves seriously. I was, essentially, the designated fool.

Felix Dennis once wrote a poem about this phenomenon and gave me a signed original at a bar. Here it is:

THE FOOL

My friend would ask me, curious,
When we were lads in school,
"You know it makes 'em furious,
Why play the bloody fool?"

My mother she would scold me
Or lecture me in tears;
How many times she told me
To emulate my peers.

When I was one and twenty,
My editor would say:
"You've talent here aplenty,
Why play the fool all day?"

And even my true lover
In gentleness will ask,
"I love you like no other,
Think you I love the mask?"

Their faces set like thunder,
The men with gravitas,
The men whose gold and plunder
Each time I play the ass—

Too late they learn their danger
In breach of fortune's rule,
That Lady Luck's a stranger
To pride, but loves a fool.

There's something about Fox I don't think anyone in this business gets. *The Five* works because they put people before politics. (Sorry to sound like a campaign ad for a local congressman, but it happens to be the truth.)

The production values are unsurpassed. They truly make us look great. I'm a stocky gremlin—and sometimes I look so good I don't recognize myself. You can stumble in hungover, eyes laden with bags the size of hacky sacks, hair sticking out all over, a busted lip and a swollen nose, and they'll turn you into a matinee idol (you should see the before pic of Jesse Watters—he makes the Elephant Man look like Ryan Gosling). The sheer effortless cohesion you see when you're watching us at home—for so many people behind the scenes, it's actually hard work and dedication that make it seem that effortless. For someone ignorant of this for so long, it became a humbling experience. I mean, I came from magazines! That's an industry where you put one thing out a month, and yet we acted like it was insane pressure just to meet one deadline a month. "Oh dear, I have to stay past seven p.m.! I better get a hotel room and a gram of coke!"

Magazines had staffs that dwarfed that of *The Five*'s, yet there we were pumping out this magical creature every day. Sort of like Hilaria Baldwin. And if I'm not there, or Dana or Jesse isn't there, the thing still rumbles on—confident in its machinery, because the machinery is there, well oiled and designed for comfort and fun.

Now I sound like an ad for the newest vibrator.

The Next Flip: Late-Night TV

It's been a decade since *The Five* (launched in 2011) and I'm doing *The Greg Gutfeld Show* (launched in 2015) as a weekly. And it's kicking ass.

So the conversation had to start again. About going nightly. That means me doing two shows a day. A bigger footprint. A bigger target. A bigger workload. But also a bigger paycheck. To say that doesn't matter would make me a liar.

Around 2021, things started percolating again.

The Greg Gutfeld Show was a hit on Saturday nights—often doubling and tripling the competition in cable news at 11 p.m. Tyrus had built a following that exploded, and Kat was coming into her own as a charming intellect—a perfect face for libertarianism (at least five decades younger than Ron Paul, and with better hair extensions).

We were building a great team. Tom O'Connor was the producer. He'd work with me at *Red Eye* and understood my humor. But more important, he understood my brain—that what might not seem funny to many would end up growing on them like an obnoxious fungus. You just need to let it breathe, like a fine wine or a gagged hostage. It might offend people straight off, but then they'd see that it's only crossing boundaries that really weren't boundaries to begin with. You just thought they were.

Finding Tyrus was truly miraculous. Here's this big pro wrestler tagging me on Twitter, for something I had said (or the reverse). I can't remember the back-and-forth because if I'm on Twitter, I'm drunk. But it caused me to take action—which I rarely do. I went on YouTube and looked him up. I thought, *This guy seems different. I want to meet him.* It had nothing to do with the tight singlet.

This is how I always hire people.

I hired Andy Levy for *Red Eye* because he'd been leaving great comments on my blog at the profoundly pretentious Huffington Post. On any given day, among hundreds of writers and blog posts, it was Levy's weird words in the comments section that rang out as the funniest.

I hired Bill Schulz because he was free and hanging around, and I don't mean in my kitchen at 3 a.m., naked, pissing in my crock pot.

He was a gifted writer and hilarious—an oddball who just needed to be pointed in the right direction. He was the opposite of commercially viable: he looked homeless and acted like a drag queen minus the drag. But if you let him loose, you couldn't take your eyes off him. He remains one of the funniest people I've ever met.

I hired Gene Nelson (you know, the tall, handsome fellow from our skits) because he sent me a binder full of ideas. Straight out of Arkansas, you know, the mecca for TV comedy—no references, no contacts. But I was impressed that someone would do this—sending me a thing as thick as an old phone book— especially when no one knows what I mean when I say "old phone book!" I took the binder home, and in it weren't just ideas for skits, but introductions for guests (often the hardest thing to come up with), as well as analysis of sets, hundreds of pics of dwarf body builders, and other stuff. Later on when he was a regular on the show, he actually presented me with the research paper he had done (without prompting—I know! what a teacher's pet, right?) on the effects of colors of objects on people observing them—and wrote a thoughtful analysis on how these colors work. I think I read half of it, not because it wasn't interesting but because reading while jet-skiing can be dangerous—but I admired the hard work and intellect behind the work. (Maybe we should give him his own cubicle now.)

Point is, I don't sift through résumés. I go for the people who are ready to work and offer something you can't find anywhere else. I also like people who take risks, which is why I can't figure out how me and Kilmeade are friends. This guy's safer than a condom on a condom.

When I reached out to Tyrus, he was wrestling, but agreed to come on the show.

He was an instant hit, largely due to a long soliloquy on being pulled over by a cop, from the perspective of a heavily tattooed black man. He allowed the viewers to sit in his place, as that large black man, when the police approached. He revealed poignantly how he prepared himself so the officer—whom

Tyrus empathized with, in his role approaching someone like Tyrus—would feel less inclined to tase him. The segment was a huge hit.

It was clear Tyrus had to be a regular. We had to hire him. Honestly, he said he'd fuck us all up in the parking garage after the show if we didn't. I told him I didn't appreciate that kind of language, so he picked me up and threw me into a dumpster . . . to which I responded, "Apology accepted." The rest is history.

Kat was a similar tale.

I got to know her through her writing at *National Review*. Her pieces were succinct serious takes on campus politics and culture. She was in her early twenties, but she wrote like a seasoned cat lady. Her personality, however, was missing from these pieces—so I had no idea what I was in for. When she showed up for her first time at *Red Eye*, I was surprised. I had seen her in a tiny picture, so I paid little attention to what kind of person she might appear to be in person. She turned out to be a lanky blonde with a voice that was a hybrid of Bea Arthur's and Fred Gwynne's, if they both were three-packs-a-day smokers. I'd never met anyone with a voice lower than hers, lead singers of Scandinavian death metal bands included.

But with every topic she would answer each question with facts, but also some wisdom you wouldn't expect from someone in their early twenties. Plus she came fully loaded with self-deprecation, which is a number one requirement for the show. She became an instant favorite, and over time blossomed into an astute confident presence on the *Gutfeld Show*, and later the nightly version. Her ability to put up with me is a credit to her confidence. And for those of you who think my insults toward her are too mean, don't forget that she writes a lot of them—in fact some of the sharpest barbs about her are written by her. Luckily for me, she really hates herself . . .

My theory of the popularity of these shows comes in stages.

Red Eye was a perfect example: First you hated it. Then it confused you. Then you adored it. Repulsion; confusion; obsession. If I made fragrances, those would be the names of my only three products. I can see the ad. Opens on me shirtless; the camera pans back to a wider shot of me, on my knees, throwing up in a toilet, then pans back to an even wider shot to reveal a large painting of Brian Stelter hanging on the bathroom wall. End of ad.

The show just kept growing and growing—especially as the news kept getting weirder and weirder.

We invented new things, some that floundered, others that were pure genius. We were building a fan base of smart folks, both young and old. Word of mouth collided with the sheer humorlessness of our competition, and over time we became appointment viewing, not simply for my old *Red Eye* audience (breastfeeding moms, graveyard shifters, and meth heads), but newbies, too (breastfeeding, graveyard-shifting meth heads).

When I had asked Tom O'Connor to come with me from *Red Eye* to do *The Greg Gutfeld Show* in 2015, I told him, this will only be weekly for a few years, because nightly is the goal.

He was one of our best producers at Fox, a former minor-league baseball player who, against stereotype, had the skewed sense of humor that athletes lack. He also could figure out a skit from the kernel of an idea in no time, produce and direct it, and have it show-ready in an hour. Most of all, he knew how to deal with me, including moments when I could not readily articulate my vision for something. Oddly, for some reason, he understood what I was trying to get at, even if I sucked trying to explain it. Also, he knew how to defuse a tantrum by laughing at me without making me feel misunderstood.

Let's just say he laughs a lot.

I told him, "We'll be nightly in no time." I was honest when I said it, but inside I was dreading the idea.

Flipping Cancel Culture

The fact is, I hated enlarging my media footprint.

But then Perino said something filled with smarts and wisdom that changed my outlook forever. She said, "You know what they say about a man with a big media footprint?" And bang, from that moment on I was all in for where this show could lead me . . . that's right, more expensive massage parlors! Anyway, the truth was I liked where I was. Being the class clown/cranky wisdom tooth of *The Five* for five days a week, and then on the sixth day, just hanging out with friends for an hour doing my own show—it was perfect!

What more could I ask for, especially when no one cared about me, really? I could still wander around the city, without being egged or beaten up—which was a regular thing for Jesse Watters. And that was *before* he was on Fox.

It was a good gig that provided enough work for me, and plus, even though I had plenty of people who wanted to cancel me, they didn't want to cancel me that badly yet. They didn't take me seriously—which is how I preferred it.

I preferred it that way: to stay under the radar (which comes easy to me) and do my work.

But that couldn't last forever. Leading up to the 2020 election, Fox News' CEO Suzanne Scott would gently prod me every two months with a meeting or a call, suggesting we start seriously considering the move to nightly. I finally had to open up to her about my concerns.

"I don't want my life ruined." We had just gone through five years of cancel culture, on top of the MeToo movement—which began as a legit and necessary campaign to rid the offices of creeps but had turned into a relentless revenge engine that provided juicy stories for reporters who weren't being yet canceled themselves. The machine was self-perpetuating, gobbling up men and spitting out their careerless husks; the accusers were rarely questioned. It sounds like old news now, but due process became thoroughly unnecessary, to be replaced by the rabid and rapid court of public opinion. The worst part, obviously, was that there was no way to defend yourself—"believe all women" made that impossible (oddly, now it's "men who say they are women"). The fear of being the next target kept everyone underground in their own psychological bomb shelters. A few of us would speak up.

But for the time being the MeToo/cancel-culture steamroller created plenty of news to cover—and cover quite easily. All you had to do was report on an alleged victim, and since she had to be believed, no follow-up was necessary. As a lowly blogger, you knew your plate was full the moment you woke up—you didn't have to think of what to write, just who to destroy.

I had three older sisters—so I know pretty damn well that sordid, gross men exist.

If I were them and had to put up with some of the crap men subjected them to, I would have made the jump to the other team quicker than you could say Chaz Bono.

But the targets expanded to include comedians with terrible game; dudes who cheated on partners (which was now called "emotionally abusive"); and consensual workplace dalliances reconfigured as abuses of the power structure. The fact is, there are supercreeps everywhere; that's for certain. I reported on them. But now, because of the pureeing of accusations, the equating of a crass and wrong comment with actual physical assault turned the real issue into a travesty. Worse, a joke. And that, believe me, doesn't upset me as much as it upset true victims of harassment—of which there were more than a few.

The targets expanded again—it was no longer just about male/female abuses, but words and jokes and old tweets. The belief that words are violence made every person a potential victim or a potential victimizer. There was no expiration date on the words one might have used, because there they were, in permanence, on the web—voluntarily served up to the masses.

If you were a liberal, you were safe from losing a career. Joy Reid had a blog full of bigoted stuff that would have made Archie Bunker wince—which she initially claimed had been hacked (the stuff was so bad, she literally pretended she had not written it). Then when it became clear that she not only wrote the stuff, but lied about it, and tried to blame others, she was fired.

JK.

No, she wasn't. Not even close. Her career has continued on. She had liberal privilege—which she exercised nightly as she called anyone on the other side politically a racist.

I knew these exceptions would never be there for me. If I stepped in something bad, I'd go down.

And I worked at Fox, meaning 98 percent of the media would love to see me go down in a blaze of fiery humiliation.

Luckily, though, I also worked . . . at Fox: I soon got the impression they would stand by me through thick and thin—provided whatever skeletons in my closet were Halloween decorations.

To paraphrase Donald Trump, I'm no angel. Not even close. And my career has ample evidence of offensive things—in fact it's all there, in magazine pages, on video, and so on. But when I say "offensive," I say that word in its current meaning—as in it carries no meaning at all.

I have yet to meet anyone who has ever been truly offended by anything said by anyone else. Even when I thought I was offended, and said so, if you came up to me and asked, "Are you really offended, Greg?" I would pause, and realize, "Uh, not really. In fact, no, not at all." I made this point in *The Joy of Hate* years ago: We aren't really feeling genuine outrage when we are outraged. We are enjoying the rush of energy from the simulation of outrage. We've created a new lymphatic system: outrage endorphins. (I love science jargon.)

I believe I can conjure up any emotion I want. If I want anger, I can go to Twitter and read something, anything. But that's on me for going there. So I try not to. And really, the only things that anger me are my own deficiencies, not others'. I get madder at myself than people I truly can't stand, because they aren't worth the effort. But I am.

My career is punctuated by things that are meant to be funny by the sheer shock of expression. It's not being a shock jock—it's just speaking things that you think, knowing that others might think the same thing. Or, once you let them hear it, they go, "Holy hell, that's insane, and it's so insane, it's funny, and I think the same thing."

Now here's what makes my career different from comedians, or edgy journalists, or rock stars—and other risk-takers. They do their stuff in appropriate venues: they tell their sick jokes in clubs, they write their pieces for so-called "edgy" publications, they write morbid lyrics for grindcore, catering to a specific kind of fan.

I did none of that. I was just as demented as they are—in fact worse at times. But I did all of it in mainstream arenas. I was editor for *Men's Health*, for God's sake—a magazine almost exclusively dedicated to abs. Some of the stuff I put in that magazine was so cutting-edge that it got me fired. Both

Stuff and *Maxim* were mass-market men's magazines—selling products to young dudes. So the content had to be, of course, all babes, beer, and gadgets. Except this editor (me) flipped it entirely, introducing ghoulish and unnerving features, and undermining the bro humor that had come to represent lazy men's magazine's editors. When I edited *Stuff*, *Maxim* was on another floor. The contrast was stark. *Stuff* was full of subversive brains writing bitingly hilarious copy about the industry they worked in, mocking its clichés. Meanwhile, *Maxim* was full of blockheads who foolishly thought their readers were as dumb as they were. *Maxim* was truly unfunny; *Stuff* broke boundaries. There's no one from *Maxim* you've ever heard from again. Meanwhile, *Maxim UK*, which I also edited, had a staff that was every bit as devious and subversive as *Stuff*, and many of them have written award-winning books, hosted shows, and gone on to marked success. One of them is currently my cleaning lady.

Then I ended up at Fox, the largest cable news network in the country. It leans right, it's pro-religion, pro-traditional, pro-military. And they give me a time slot at 2 a.m., then 3 a.m. to create a show. *Red Eye*, without a doubt, was the strangest hour of television, period. And it was made stranger because it was on a mainstream network.

If *Red Eye* happened to be on Comedy Central, you could actually make sense of that. Or if it were on MTV. But Fox News?

How could that happen? Why would that happen? It made no sense.

So there you have it—every risk I took was not in an area where it seemed appropriately housed. I was taking risks in a risk-averse neighborhood. And I didn't think twice about it. It's one thing to test-drive sex dolls for Vice, but it's another to do it at a mainstream magazine.

As I watched people getting canceled, I would sit up at night and think about all the shit I wrote, all the features I commissioned. It overwhelmed me. Think John Wayne Gacy with an English degree. I trafficked in the sick, the morbid, and the dead. I was a descendant of Gahan Wilson, *National Lampoon*, the Cramps, *Fernwood Tonight*, and Chris Elliot all rolled into one smarmy stentorian showman.

How long before they would revisit my past? Some started doing that once *The Five* really took off. They dug up old tweets. When I saw them, though, they never seemed as bad as I thought they'd be. Perhaps I had the tendency of exaggerating my own risk-taking. Maybe I was safer than I thought! Or maybe my "vice" signaling prepared everyone for who I already was.

You have to remember: at this time, say 2014 to 2020, people actually had to take the social media scalp hunters seriously because everyone was petrified of being next.

The scalpers had something people like me didn't have:

time. Like me when I broke into Perino's apartment while she was out of town—they could spend all day looking through my dirty laundry (thank God, metaphorically, I wore the same shirt and pants every day).

Luckily, every day on my shows, I would display my dirty laundry—the drug use, the deviance, the sick humor—so when they would find some dirt about me ("He did cocaine!!"), I would laugh and let them know I talked about that more times in public than anyone I know. Before I got married, I was a drinker, a druggie, slept around, got into brawls. There's nothing about that I haven't hid. Except maybe my dungeon. But that stays between me and Pat Sajak. So it's especially funny when someone thinks they got me—when I got me first. Like I said, it's called vice signaling. (Try it, you'll like it. Vice signaling is now my central vice.)

It's a sound strategy, a preemptive strike against cancellation that creates a protective moat from miserable busybodies. Except I never planned it that way. I just did it because it was true, and fun.

But now, if I had to give advice for people with a past, it would be to talk about it. Just not to me—I'm far too busy with my macramé.

Still, when I considered expanding my exposure, I had to factor in that I would piss off people more than ever. Especially people in the media who hated my success already. What if I were to double it? Would the media hacks devote whole staffs to tracking down exes and old posts? Probably.

It actually bothered me, that I cared. I hated myself for caring.

Someone joked during all of this that there must be plenty of influential, powerful men lying awake at nights in a cold sweat.

My problem: I was neither influential nor powerful, but being neurotic meant I would still lie awake. That, and because Taylor Swift snores.

Sometimes I would tell a coworker about this and they weren't much help. "Well, I don't have that problem," one woman said. I had to remind her that she was married, and has sons and brothers—so, yes, if those men ever had a problem, she'd have a problem, because it happens not to you, but to the people who love you. So it does happen to you, too.

My point: even if you have a clean, boring past, you can bet someone you love doesn't. And if you're in the public—so are they.

When I agonized over going nightly I told my wife, Elena, "I don't need the trouble, Elena." She said, "There's nothing that they can say about you that you haven't said already about your-self."

It's really a very astute analysis.

I hoped she was right, but I was betting I was wrong.

So I told Suzanne that maybe I wasn't the guy for this.

She seemed a little bemused, but remained patient, thankfully.

She didn't get on the phone and call for her second choice (Brad Pitt).

Then a few things happened.

The 2020 election, for one, which meant Biden would be president, and even better, Kamala Harris would be VP. Like each new strain of Covid, it was really a terrible gift that would not stop giving. As much as the Trump presidency provided nightly entertainment—he being funnier than all the late-night hosts—a Biden presidency would need someone like me. Because none of the other guys or gals were gonna touch him.

He was their guy. And they were so relieved to be rid of Trump—even though he was their only punch line. With that punch line gone, what was left?

Colbert doing a musical number praising the vaccine.

Comedy at night was no longer comedy: it was propaganda thinly disguised as entertainment.

But it wouldn't be just the White House bringing a much-needed new target for sarcasm and ridicule. Along with their arrival would come other assorted wackjob hires and absurd policies, all driven by the most ridiculous movement in modern history: wokeism.

What is wokeism? I'll quote Wilfred Reilly here, a badass, extremely fearless black professor, courtesy of Twitter:

Wokeism is the belief that (1) all of society is currently and intentionally structured to oppress, (2) all gaps in performance between large groups illustrate this, and (3) the solution is "equity"—proportional representation w/o regard to performance.

That's a pretty naked assessment. And I'm a big fan of naked. Ask the young couple who live in the apartment building that looks down on my balcony.

But you can add this, from me:

There is no way to fix the system wokeism condemns. The system is not just currently structured to oppress: it will always be the case. So the system must be destroyed.

It exists in every part of the American landscape: from the workplace to entertainment to law and order.

There is no limit to how you can destroy it. You can use mob tactics, violence, doxing, you name it. It's really up to you, because you're in a war against the oppressor. Everyone is racist, and racism is worse than pedophilia. Especially since the most vocal wokesters now defend pedophiles—calling them "minor-attracted persons."

> It's very easy to adopt as a practice. Lacking complexity or nuance, you can apply it anywhere like cheap spray paint. If you're an enterprising shameless writer, you can create a dartboard featuring all these areas of life. Throw a dart, and where it hits, you just take that topic and add "How (movies, nursing, comedy, automobiles, seafood, etc.) is systematically corrupted by white privilege."

This stuff was spreading through the media like a novel virus because the media had no immune system or spine. Not just because they are cowards (which they are), but also because they'd been infiltrated by social justice warriors—generally flocking to noncreative positions in various large companies. They were there to fuck with the product, not create or improve it. To live off of it as it kills it. A sort of corporate tapeworm. Everyone adopted the same stance: to be scared of them. So they were.

I saw it bubbling up like monkeypox. I'd seen it before when it was just "Everything is racist" a decade ago. Now it was "Everything is oppressive." If you didn't agree, then you were part of the oppressiveness. It allowed for all sorts of down-punching in the media, and real punching on the streets. CNN would send reporters to visit citizens at their homes who might have posted a right-wing meme. People would actually attack Trump supporters on their way to rallies. Asian women were being sucker-punched for reasons that only had to do with their own industriousness (they're out walking to and from work, taking the subway, minding their own business). They were successful, and for that—they were oppressive.

Someone had to call this out and also make fun of this humorless, dangerous stuff. The thing is, I had been doing that for a while, but my target didn't have a common name yet.

Back in the day, I used to end my *Red Eye* monologues with "And if you disagree with me, you're a racist homophobe." That was fifteen years ago. I was only kidding. But I was predicting the way the world was going, and sure enough, that's exactly where it went. I'm like Nostradamus! But with underpants and a manicure.

Wokeism preached a divisive ideology pitting people against each other, by splitting them into two groups—oppressor versus oppressed. Then it decided that its biggest offender was humor. There was nothing funny anymore about being funny. Because in the filter of oppressor versus oppressed, the joke teller is always the oppressor.

I'd been writing about cancel culture and identity politics a lot (see *The Joy of Hate* and *Not Cool*), and wokeism combined both into a new virulent neo-McCarthyism that vowed to punish anyone who didn't obey.

Perhaps this is the reason the late-night comedians wouldn't touch it. They didn't want the hassle, and they didn't like people like me who had gotten there first in the counterattack. Oh, they loved the spotlight, but not that kind of spotlight. I totally understood that. But I wasn't going to let it stop me from pointing out that Lia Thomas is swimming against women half her size, and beating them like a Karen mouthing off at a Waffle House in Atlanta at two in the morning.

So there's that. And the 2020 election meant that all late-night shows had to shift from bashing Trump to . . . what, exactly? They couldn't bash the Democrats, ever. So somehow, if it were even possible, they would become less funny than they ever were before. I mean, during the Trump years, they made their livings off one joke (orange man bad), leaving all their tiny comedy muscles to atrophy. There was no way they would be up to the job of entertaining the rest of America.

I could hear that challenge screaming at me like a homeless man outside my window (in New York, it could have been an actual homeless man, or Keith Olbermann—likely the same thing).

I started feeling something inside.

My balls were returning. (It was either that or an inguinal hernia.) They had, for lack of a better term, "taken their own vacation from the culture wars."

But I could see that this was free money, figuratively and literally, left on the table. I was perfectly situated to enter late-night TV and run that table—and even knock my competitors off their little chairs, for good. Yet, I didn't know what to do.

So, first, I called a few friends. One veteran talk show host agreed with my fears and initial assumptions—that I had a nice gig, and should stick with it. You don't need the headaches. He presented my life exactly how I saw it, and why in hell would I want to ruin that. Plus, it's just a ton of work to do a late-night show, on top of *The Five*. As you get older, Greg, I would say to myself, you should be working less, not more. It all made sense, and I felt great. I decided that was the right thing to do. And I felt strongly about it. A weight had been lifted off my shoulders. I returned to the macramé.

Until I called Tucker. I don't know why I called him, frankly. Maybe because I trusted him. Also, he really doesn't give a single fuck, period. He's more right than wrong on things, being always ahead of the curve. He's made me rethink my own positions, not only in my career, but in the bedroom. The secret move he taught me makes me one of the top ten lovers in the nation if not the world. I won't get into it here, but he calls it "the bow tie." Anyway, enough about that!

He's said some things to me that have stayed with me forever. Like, "How'd you get my number?" and "Whatever you do, if you mention my name to the police I will kill you with my bare hands."

One time in the greenroom we were debating the necessity for the Transportation Security Administration and the Patriot Act. I was on the side of keeping both, and Tucker was like, "No, Greg—it's wrong, and it has to go." I said the most obvious response: "I don't want to die in a terrorist attack."

He said, "You won't. But if you did, what a way to go." He reframed my thinking right there.

So I called Tucker, foolishly thinking he'd agree that I didn't need another burden. Another hassle. But when I told him what the other famous comedian guy had told me, Tucker unleashed his trademark out-of-control laugh and exclaimed: "Are you insane??? You have to do this, Gutfeld! You have to do this!" That's pretty much all it took.

Then I think he hung up on me—probably to go jogging while chomping on nicotine gum. I only say that because it's my best memory of Tucker: As I left a bar in Midtown one night after last call, I ran into him in gray sweats running down Forty-Seventh Street, chewing his gum, sweating. This was around 1 a.m. And get this, nobody was chasing him! Man, how New York has changed. I improved my time in the 5K simply by sprinting nightly from Fox News to the subway! (I kid. I have a chauffeur, and we run together.)

So, for some reason, when Tucker tells you that while laughing, he's telling me more than just "Do it." He is looking at it as fun; it's an adventure. You should want to do it sheerly out of curiosity. It's this mentality that kills his adversaries—there's literally nothing you can do to him that penetrates his innate happiness.

Also, and most important, don't take yourself so seriously.

It was the same logic he had offered about the TSA. Gutfeld, you can't walk around in fear, anticipating the worst. Because if the worst truly happens, it beats dying of cancer. (That's my interpretation, having seen my dad die from it over a period of years.)

Nobody has ever lain on their deathbed, saying, "I should have done less shit, tried less shit, and lived life to the emptiest!" Well, maybe Led Zeppelin's drummer, John Bonham, but nobody else.

It's a problem I've had most of my life. I don't have a curiosity about the future, I have a fear of it. That's anxiety, I guess, by definition. I actually looked it up (that counts as research, and therefore makes me a scholar and I get to deduct the meds).

I almost never think of the present. I don't even know if that's possible.

But I think about the past, as a creator of possible disasters in the future. So my life is a bouncing ball between those two sectors: past and future, back and forth.

The present moment never really exists, because it always ends the moment you address it, so I take real risks constantly with my unpredictable mouth.

But because of my risk-taking, I become worried by the

things I might have done in the past, and how they will disrupt the future. When I forget the past, I might still be terrified of what happens next. It takes a lot for me to go out and actually do things that most people consider fun.

I was never like this. I was adventurous . . . but it was only because I had no other choice.

I moved from San Francisco to Allentown with nothing really in my pocket, not because I wanted to live the life of a blue-collar hipster in the heart of steel country, but because I was broke. I had no choice. (Well, that and Billy Joel made it sound so cool in that song!)

That is totally appropriate when you're in your early twenties. You can't wait for the ideal option; you have to go where the option is.

That's how my life—from a psychological progression—unfolds.

It's embarrassing but true: my quest for success—and the wealth and comfort it brings—was entirely to cocoon myself from the causes of my anxieties.

The more money I made, the less you saw of me. I moved to a cabin. I ordered my meals in, instead of going out. I stopped going to bars unless I had a specific place to sit and a reliable waiter I knew by name. I never went to movies anymore. I was in a Covid lockdown five years before Covid hit. Money was designed to protect me from my relentless worries. When I'm watching a real-life story on TV about a bunch of people who died in an avalanche after attempting to heli-ski an untouched mountain, I pull the afghan up a little tighter, readjust my pillow, and belly laugh . . . Hey, honey, more pretzels, please! Sorry, it just makes me feel brighter than them.

Luckily I am surrounded by people who pry me out of this, in novel ways.

I remember being on the road, doing live shows with Tom Shillue, and he was interested in checking out the city we happened to be in, by foot. It was rainy and grimy and I had mentioned that I didn't want the hassle. He reframed my anxiety by turning it into curiosity. "Don't you want to see what's out there? Greg, life is an adventure!" He said this with his eyes almost popping out of his head. He was right. Then we got mugged.

Be a Potato

So: "Don't you want to see what's next?"

Once you flip your filter from dread to curiosity, everything changes.

Sadly, my filter was often clogged with dread . . . the "lint" that blocks curious thought, I guess.

A very successful friend of mine had a suggestion. "If you want to distract your mind, do something you wouldn't normally do just to see how it turns out. Make yourself curious and your other problems will shrink in your mind from neglect." I took this as testing your expertise with prediction and probability.

It's true. I mean you can take it to extremes. Like if I have a headache, it goes away the moment I stub my toe. But if you're concerned over someone at work talking shit about you, maybe it's not a bad thing to go to a museum, or try to cook something you never cooked. I once roasted an entire wildebeest because Dana said one of my jokes didn't land.

But I started to lose that dread filter.

I started to stop acting like my life was really that precious. Sure, I had to take care of myself (and I do), but I didn't have to act like I was some fragile Fabergé egg that must be kept from the rough streets and alleys of a crime-ridden city.

My friend (whose name rhymes with Clot Madams) reframes it this way: In one of his podcasts he asks you to imagine that someone asked you to carry a potato across the street from your place to some other destination. No problem, it's just a potato. But imagine if that someone asked you to carry a priceless Picasso across the street to the same place. The anxiety and fear explode. What about crime? The weather? Birds pooping?

Right now, I'm trying to change my filter—from thinking that I'm carrying a Picasso, to instead carrying a potato. In fact, when I'm about to do something I'm dreading, I say to myself, "Be a potato." That instantly devalues myself. I'm no longer fragile. I still watch for traffic, and don't drive without a seat belt—but my agoraphobic nature has been eased, at least when I remember to be a potato. It must be easy for my old pal, being bald and seventy, to do this exercise, since he actually looks like a potato.

So, as a potato, and not a painting, I realized I could handle just about anything.

At first I really wasn't convinced it was gonna work, so I made some adjustments to his idea and tried that. I pretended I was carrying a painting of a potato done by Hunter Biden. I was trying to split the difference between the value of a potato and a Picasso, but it didn't really work and just made me crave whiskey and curly fries.

I was nothing special, and the world was a subjective universe that we, as potatoes, perceive differently. When I was faced with doing things that filled me with angst—filming a Super Bowl ad or appearing on Bill Maher's podcast—I became a potato. And <u>it worked</u>.

So, after the election, humor was nowhere to be found in that late-night desert. The news certainly seemed grim. The unfunny people stayed unfunny. In fact, they got more and more earnest—the death knell of comedy. I needed to be less of a Picasso, and more of a potato. But a bold, russet, Idaho potato—not some dinky little red potato like in the buffet at Cracker Barrel. Those are potatoes, right?

So we were living in crazy times, with Covid and crime, and woke mobs chasing down anyone who didn't bend to their hysterical demands—and there needed to be a response.

That response had to be me. I mean, who else could it be?

Credit: FOX News

No.

I called Suzanne and said, "Yes, it's time, you're right, we have to do this, and we have to do it now!" She was like, "Thank you for coming around, you silly jerk. Now, remind me who you are again?"

And we got to work.

We picked a date (April 5) and decided to tinker around with concepts and set design and guests, and segments. My feeling was not to overthink anything. Just jump in the pool and start swimming, and sooner or later, the stuff figures itself out. That's how *The Five* worked.

What makes a show successful? I'm sure other people will offer different opinions, but I'm pretty confident it comes down to these two secret sauces:

- Chemistry: if we don't get along, then it's awkward and tedious. For a good example of the anti-*Five*, watch any panel show on any other network. It's grim. They make the Nuremberg Trials look like *Family Feud*. (CNN's disastrous morning show with Don Lemon proved this point.)

- Teasing: if you can't make fun of the person you're with, then that means the first requirement (chemistry) doesn't exist. The moment I started making fun of Dana, and Bob Beckel made fun of me, and so on, we knew the show was a hit.

Try this experiment in your life: Separate the people into two groups (not counting bosses). Split them into who you can tease, and people you can't. You'll see it instantly: the people you tease, you genuinely *love*. The people you can't tease, you loathe.

So I kept the construction of the new late night show simple: keep it close to the structure of our Saturday product; just add more guests and see what happens.

When I broke the news to Kat and Tyrus, I told them that things were about to change in a big way—not just for each of us individually (they would both become bigger stars); for us it would also mean becoming a more cohesive, intertwined, and tease-happy group.

We would now see each other every day, and that was going to have a massive impact on us in terms of chemistry. I never really made fun of either of them—after all, we only had an hour together—but now the time spent in each other's company would be multiplied by five, and what would happen?

We would become so comfortable with each other that we would roast each other as our preferred form of communication. We would find things out about each other and poke at those things. Or, if you're like me, totally make stuff up about them. I told Kat that I needed to create a persona based on her own persona. She is a good girl, but she's also willing to try anything. Her basic mantra is "Let's fucking go!" Most important, and she would agree about this: she's a dude, full of masculine energy and a guy's voice—who happens to be a woman. So that was the persona I would amplify. Likewise, Tyrus did the same to me: he took my obvious eccentricities (my inclination toward potty humor and nonsensical flights of verbal perversion) and registered his disgust. He hammered me on it nightly. These connections would be building every night, and get stronger and deeper—and before you knew it, we worked seamlessly like a three-piece bar band who'd played at a club every night for years.

That's why we took this picture at Nashville, Tennessee, when we were about to start doing a week of shows before a large audience in a bar . . .

Kat, Tyrus, and Greg from Gutfeld's first road show at the
Listening Room Cafe in Nashville, Tennessee.
Credit: Gabrielle Penner

This is not the typical picture you'd see of TV or even Fox talent.

This is the type of picture you'd find in a press release about Aerosmith's first album, the self-titled one with "Dream On," circa 1973. First, it's black-and-white. In every sense. We were all scowling and staring directly at you (or perhaps the competition), presenting a united, intriguing, and appealing front. We were all different parts of the same well-oiled band.

Tyrus was the massive monument of sheer intellectual intensity: God help you if he directed his brain, if not his brawn, in your direction. Kat was the sharpest knife in the cutlery drawer, and more wiry than the cables under your office monitors. And there's the demented but determined mascot, me—who directs the mayhem as if he knows where all of this is headed. Usually, I don't.

Then I considered guests. The topic of celebrities came up. I needed to dispel the myth that they are the main ingredient for success. They aren't.

Sure, they can be a big draw—even I'd watch Colbert if he had, say, Morrissey on (I'm a big Doors fan). I'd watch Kimmel if I knew he snagged Clint Eastwood (I'm a fan of his singing in *Paint Your Wagon*).

But 99 percent of the time, most celebrities are delivered to talk shows in invisible cages. They're told what to say, and what not to say. And the hosts are fine with it. It's not like they want to know what Ryan Reynolds thinks about interest rates (by the way, no one wants to know what anyone thinks about interest rates—sorry, Kudlow).

I'd been through this kind of thing before. When I edited *Stuff*, you had to trade puff pieces for interviews and cover spreads. If we wanted J-Lo on the cover, I could only ask her about her new movie, or her new record—but never anything else. It was never about true entertainment, on behalf of the reader—but influence. It got to be pretty awful. I remember after a photo shoot thanking one big star and, as she was leaving, realizing she still had our diamond stud in her belly button. That was a fifteen-grand stud—a trifle to her, but something I had to get back or else we'd have to pay whoever supplied it for the shoot. But I decided not to bring it up. I couldn't jeopardize the relationship. So off she went with the stud, and my business guy had to call the insurance agency. I never knew what happened to that stud. Which is something often said about me.

So you had to play it safe with stars—even bad ones.

I swear, if we were able to get OJ right after the murders, we probably would have asked him about his favorite cologne (I'm guessing Obsession) and, as a widower, when would he be ready to date again. (I'm guessing his answer would have been "Whenever the wake ends.")

On *Red Eye*, we would be offered celebrities, and every once in a while I would say yes, and then instantly regret it after the show ended. One well-known actor showed up drunk as hell and lit a cigarette during the interview, unaware he was on TV, and that it was actually illegal to do so on set. He was obnoxious and sweaty. As a favor to the film company, we never aired the segment. I kinda regret that. I was too nice back then. Do you believe that? I had a chance to ruin Larry Storch's career and didn't!?

Another fading comedian showed up coked to the gills. He decided it would be hilarious to harass one well-known conservative female panelist. He was touching her, poking his finger in her face, perhaps imagining this made him seem like a hero to the Left.

After the first block, rather than boot the guy, we ended up moving the guests around the table so he could no longer intimidate the woman. The comic had come highly recommended, but he was never heard from again.

He thought his shtick would be hilarious and brave. "I'm going on Fox News to fuck with right-wingers!" He ended up looking starkly pathetic. A sad, creepy, charmless sack of shit. That's not me describing him, that's the title of his soon-to-be released autobiography.

We had some surprises with other celebrities, but they rarely made the shows better or moved the needle, ratings-wise. At best they might be mildly interesting, but they were instructed not to be. They were there not to make news, but to promote a show, or a movie.

It's the same with the other guys on late night TV. They were trading their audience for the celebrity cachet—in return the TV show might get a bump in their ratings and the celeb's movie might open bigger. For the most part the interviews would suck.

We've had some big names on our show. But so few I can rattle them off here.

John Waters. Caitlyn Jenner. Johnny Rotten. Leslie Jordan. Russell Brand. John Rich. The forty-fifth president of the United States. Those were the fun ones, to be sure.

But really, the people that intrigued me were lesser-known faces—Douglas Murray. King Buzzo. Walter Kirn. Mike Baker. The singer from Gwar.

But my formula was simple: whoever sat with us that particular evening had to be smart, and original. But most important: interesting. Because even brilliant people can be boring. It's not their fault that they didn't practice jokes in front of a mirror because they were too busy building rockets to Mars. But still, a few laughs would be a good way to break the ice with those green aliens you're going to meet.

The show was, in a way, designed to be a little cocktail party with my favorite people, and the viewers were invited. In fact, that party was being thrown for them. I knew that if I could draw the guests out of their normal comfort zone, the audience would fall in love with them the way I already had.

Many of them were already notable in their own industries, but I introduced these guests to millions of people, who saw in them what I saw, whether it was Jamie Lissow, Emily Compagno, or, again, Kirn.

Kirn is the perfect guest, the kind of person you saw growing up (if you were my age) on Merv Griffin, Mike Douglas, or Johnny Carson. It didn't matter what the topic was, or if he had a "project" to pump: when he started talking, people in your living room quieted down (you could say the same thing for Tyrus and Kat, too). Kirn wrote a number of great books, including *Up in the Air*, which was made into a critically acclaimed film starring my lookalike, George Clooney. He is a rare breed, in that you never know what will come out of his mouth, except that it will surprise you, and not by virtue of shock value, but because you would never have heard that opinion before. He lives in Montana. I contend he knows more about the state of America than anyone alive. He knows where bodies are buried, who the pedos are, and how to get good acid. In fact he has a storage of acid that is so rare, it's only shared among the precious few (it's why *Outnumbered* is so often nonsensical).

I also embraced the people who were no longer embraced by their tribe. People like Dave Rubin, Peter Boghossian, Bret Easton Ellis, Chadwick Moore. As the liberals got sucked further into the black hole of wokeism, I was the beneficiary of those sound minds who were able to escape with their brains intact. The show became the perfect place for the anti-woke and the newly canceled to come and be themselves. We were witness protection for the fleeing left. And they loved it.

Of course, to make the show come alive for the people at home, you need a live audience, in the studio.

I was never a fan of it because I was never a comedian. I wasn't used to that experience. In fact I hated going to comedy clubs, because I felt anxious for the people up onstage, and I felt anxious for myself. On more than one occasion, comedians have stared at me, and started asking me questions about stuff, and there's no way out of that. Okay, to be fair to the comics, the two times it happened I was wearing Daisy Duke shorts, shirtless, with a denim vest and a mesh baseball cap that said FUCK YOU on it.

In one club, a floundering comedian started doing crowd work and came to me. I have a hard time pretending to enjoy something, and sadly, I was tucked into a tight front row—there was no way out. He started asking me why I looked so miserable. I said, "I came here for comedy." That was the last time I went to a comedy show.

But honestly, that's all bullshit: I was just scared of an audience in front of me.

But one day roughly six years ago I was on a stair climber at some gym downtown and was writing my notes for *The Five*, and the great comedian Colin Quinn approached me, impressed that I could write while climbing. I told him I was starting a new show (the Saturday show at the time), and he offered to meet me for coffee to talk about it (he, like many comedians, doesn't drink). We met at a Starbucks and he drank two Diet Cokes and pushed for a studio audience. His explanation was simple: an audience is the only way you're ever going to get better. You need that instant response to know what works and what doesn't.

Without an audience, I could say something brilliant to complete silence, and would assume it was because there was no audience there to laugh about it. But in reality, what I said could have really sucked. I had no way of knowing, with the exception of the polite laughter coming from the floor directors (shout-out to Dave and Nina; and yes, I got your emails . . . small bills it is).

I understood what he meant. I knew that I had to get over that fear. And it turned out the fear was largely unfounded.

True, maybe I was scared to find out that none of my stuff would work! But even that fear was silly, because in time, the

feedback would help shape my improvements. I had to remind myself to "be a potato not a Picasso, be a potato not a
Picasso."

The big problem with an audience was a phenomenon I
came to find was called clapter, which originated on *The Daily
Show* and Bill Maher's *Real Time*. The audience would clap instead of laugh—a response to a political point they happened
to agree with. The clapping would feel great to the panelist de-
livering a red-meat comment, but there was no comedy there.
On *Real Time*, you could say, "Orange-man Hitler needs to go
to jail," and get wild applause—but it would still not be funny,
even to the host.

On my show, someone could say "Donald Trump is the
greatest president in history" and get the same wild applause.
Red meat all around, but it's not entertaining, even if it feels
good at the time. It's basically empty calories. I try to avoid
those moments, but I can't tell guests what to say since I've
said similar things. Instead I try to prod them to move beyond
the easy red meat—the "all liberals are mentally ill," or "Hillary
should be locked up forever"—and go deeper. If they can't, then
they won't be back on the show.

Having said that, I've been guilty of inviting clapter, but
mostly as an energy device. If I feel there's a lull in the show, I
might say something that wakes the crowd up. But I hate doing

it. It feels cheap. Too easy. Like a woman flashing her breasts on the jumbotron. Okay, okay, it's 2023—I should say a woman flashing her dick.

Of course, when Covid struck, out went the audiences, and for a good period of months, I did the show from a mobile studio. I was sitting in a van, literally in a driveway outside my house. During one massive storm, a tree fell next door and destroyed my neighbor's shiny Tesla, which sucked big-time . . . and the TV van sped off, the driver in terror (without me). He had good reason. Trees were falling like Joe Biden on the Air Force One airstairs (Red meat alert!), taking down dangerous live power lines with them. I was about to do *The Five* and it was about 4:45 p.m. when I finally figured out how to meet up with the van, which was parked outside a nearby cemetery. I snuck into another neighbor's yard and climbed a fence and ran to the van in my shorts as it poured. It's not the first time I've been seen running to a van in nothing but shorts, but the first time without a cop and two K-9s chasing me.

But if you were at home watching you would never have known. The screen behind me in the van had an image of a Fox News newsroom. Never mind that I looked like a scrubby, sweaty Ahab after tangling with a whale.

Finally we did end up back in a studio, and later, in fact, a brand-new studio that could hold one hundred audience members. It was fantastic. The applause and laughter fed the energy—and suddenly we were seeing smart, serious guests turn into bona fide laugh-getters.

Dagen McDowell, whom one might see as a serious Fox Business nerd, became a rollicking redneck with memorable descriptions for everyone. Dana Perino, who might be seen as a Miss Goody Two-shoes, revealed a sly, leering side that perhaps only her husband had seen before. Even Brian Kilmeade made people laugh (rarely).

To set the mood of the first nightly show, I actually assembled a separate panel to observe the show (with its own panel of guests) and then review it. This panel of critics were Tucker, Kilmeade, and Perino, and they ripped me to shreds (which I demanded). It told everyone that not only will we tease you, but we will tease us—more.

That was just icing on the cake.

The cake was the ratings.

We were, to put it mildly, destroying the competition.

At the 11 p.m. hour, we crushed MSNBC so badly, it likely accelerated Brian Williams's retirement (no one noticed, except for his fellow Navy SEAL teammates). CNN's Don Lemon couldn't even find viewers at the airport, where people are forced to watch.

Then there were the late-night shows. One by one we knocked them off.

Forget *The Daily Show*, Samantha Bee (another canceled casualty), then Kimmel, Fallon. In mere months we started beating Colbert like it was his gang initiation.

I knew we'd be a success, but I hadn't thought it would come this fast.

We became the kings and queens of late night. Every day when the ratings would come out for the night before, it was never bad news. Only good.

The effects were striking.

First, the critics who had given us weeks to live were now stone silent. That normally happens to cowards who, rather than admit they were wrong, just hope no one remembers what they wrote. They're usually right—because what they do for a living is utterly forgettable.

But then the general press had to start reporting . . . and the number of "Well, we can't ignore this anymore" stories about us grew. Fox's public relations people were calling us daily with interviews. For once it wasn't about something I said on *The Five* that made media reporters wet their Lululemon leggings.

There were nights when we were number one across the board at our time slot in *all* of cable. We were beating nationally televised sporting events (true, it might have been the NCAA women's lacrosse semifinals, but still), and it no longer became news that we were crushing the Jimmys.

We almost became bored of winning, as Orange-man-bad always used to say.

The success happened quickly, but none of us took it for granted.

People would come up to me and ask "How does it feel?" I would say "What?"

It wasn't that I was oblivious. I guess I just accepted this as exactly what was to be expected.

I went on my usual way, churning out content, and having fun and going home to think about the next day's monologue. Something I learned early on: always get a head start on tomorrow's work, because if you don't, your sleep will be punctuated with worry. Or bed-wetting, which, fortunately, I grew out of two years ago, thanks to Steve Doocy buying an electric blanket.

But if I know that tomorrow I will have an angle on, say, the crime wave, and hopefully a paragraph summary I wrote in between push-ups and Pinot Noir, then I was set. This is a key piece of advice: Past Greg should always do a favor for Future Greg. They are two separate people, and it's easy for PG to ignore FG, because he hasn't arrived yet. But when he arrives, and the laptop screen is empty, FG starts to really hate PG.

I had the work thing down, but I had forgotten how to deal with stuff after that. I wasn't taking success for granted, but I wasn't exploiting it, either. I should be exploiting it, in the best possible way. It wasn't until I got a call from Rob Schneider, one of the rare great comics who was enjoying my success as much as anyone, that I made a conscious effort to do so. He said this to me, and I'll never forget it: "Dude, I hope you're enjoying this. You need to." The last time I had heard that was from my dad when he walked in on me and the hooker he got me for my sixteenth birthday. (Next time, check under the hood, Dad.)

Rob was right. In a way, I had forgotten to enjoy it.

Look, I'd helmed a bunch of successful things, from *Men's Health* to *Maxim* to *Red Eye* to *The Five*. I was in my fifties, although how could you tell! I'd been around. So, I never lost sight of the fact that this was a job.

But I'd forgotten I wasn't the only one there. I have a staff. Did they have any idea what they're part of? That this sort of thing doesn't just happen . . . it's rare. (Especially in this business when you have my political bent.) For some people, hell, this kind of success never happens at all (see Hal Sparks or David Frum).

Or rather, don't see them. Because you can't. At least, not on television.

I realized that I need to remind myself and the staff to enjoy this. Go out. Brag.

Have a great time. I decided to stop being a hermit, and go out with people.

Have stupid steak dinners with absurd wine bills. (I had no idea Riunite was so pricey.) Throw parties for no reason.

I figured, at this point, if I let this slide, and treat it like another job, I will regret it for the rest of my life, like I did when I walked away from my job as Zsa Zsa Gabor's fluffer.

So I flipped myself. I went from the cranky hermit to an outgoing fool.

I decided to stay out after work and have fun again.

Now, I was used to being recognized on the street, but nothing like this.

It was all new people, new faces, new kinds of fans.

I'm not gonna lie: in New York City, being on Fox News, no matter how popular you are, you can somewhat live in obscurity. That's because the only time most New Yorkers put on FNC is when their kid swallows a household cleaner and they need to induce vomiting. Meanwhile, Don Lemon claims he gets mobbed while walking to a bodega to buy his free-range cucumbers. The only people who recognize you are tourists from Texas and some ex-cons from Rikers (sometimes those groups overlap).

But then everything flipped. I couldn't go to bars anymore (a good thing, according to my wife). I would be chased down blocks for selfies, but death threats increased exponentially. I accepted the threats, but I also reported them.

There were times before this that I would be recognized, but for the wrong reasons.

I've told this story in my live shows, but it's worth telling here.

A few years ago I was sitting in a bar at an airport, waiting for my wife to arrive from somewhere far away. I was playing with my phone, and every time I looked up, I saw an older man glaring at me from behind his tall beer. Like Kilmeade, he was older—in his sixties—and it was clear he had something on his mind. I assumed it would only be a matter of time before he came over and gave me a piece of it. And he did.

After fifteen minutes of persistent glaring, he finally got up and walked over. *Here it comes*, I think. Shaking, with a tremble in his voice, too, he says, "You, sir, should be ashamed of what you do for a living." Okay, fine, I think . . . another Fox hater. Maybe he'll stop now. But when I said nothing back, he added, "TMZ has ruined so many lives."

Then he stormed off.

I was not so much confused as I was angry. How in God's name could he mistake me for Harvey Levin? It would have made more sense to me if he had said "I thought you sucked in *Turner & Hooch*!" or "You, sir, should be ashamed of what you do for a living. What kind of name is 'the Rock' anyway?"

But now, with the success of *Gutfeld!* I was being recognized for being me. Which has its ups and downs.

I get more fans assailing me on the street, which is an ego boost, for sure. But I also get crazies who threaten to kill me. One is currently doing a few years in federal prison for doing just that. (I hope Biden doesn't get wind of this or he'll pardon Tom

Arnold.) Another freak sent me an envelope of white powder—and sadly, it wasn't the stuff you can snort. Turns out it wasn't anthrax, either, but they had to vacate the entire twenty-first floor at Fox. It needed it, frankly, after ten years of Jesse's cologne.

A massive squad of officers in white jumpsuits showed up, and for once they weren't there to take Kat to Bellevue Hospital. They quarantined me. Took me to a bathroom and took all my clothes. They also made me wash myself at the sink. I couldn't return to my office, and spent hours in lockdown. The entire stretch of Sixth Avenue outside our building was blocked with fire trucks and police cruisers. I lost count of the different uniforms pacing around the offices. (And I'm not even including the police strip-o-gram we ordered for Ainsley Earhardt's birthday.)

Turns out it was baking soda. The last time I saw an overreaction like that to baking soda was when my mom made a lemon pound cake, and my dad called a SWAT team.

Even though the authorities were able to track down the origin of the sender (through the purchase of the stamp for the envelope), they said it would be almost impossible to prove. Anyone could have used that stamp, after all.

But that's the price of success, I guess. You attract weirdos who hate your success. Like what if I told you that the person who allegedly might have sent that envelope happened to be a would-be but terrible comedian? Of course, I'd never say that.

Well, technically, I can't say that. Since no one has been arrested.

Flipping Hollywood

I get asked this question a lot from college kids. Aside from what hotel I'm staying at, they ask: How do I respond to people who outnumber me on campus and trash me for my beliefs?

My answer: Just say "Do you ever wonder why I'd choose the harder path? Why would I make it hard on myself? I mean, I could just do what *you* are doing. So aren't you curious as to why I would make myself less popular rather than more?" It's a question I posed to my evaporating competition. *Do you ever wonder why we aren't doing you?* The answer isn't as important as them hearing that question . . .

True. People in my industry don't like us. We don't repeat the accepted platitudes. Before, you gotta understand, I was just harmless. They could pat me on the head and say "He just doesn't know any better." But when the winning begins, suddenly they don't want you around anymore. They'll marginalize your ideas. They'll say that you used to be funny, but not anymore. They don't want to face you. Maybe because I knew then better than they did. They don't want to have to fight for their beliefs. Perhaps because they're less confident in them as the tide changes. So, we must all agree. Or the cocktail party sucks. What a chickenshit way to go through life, especially in this industry.

Yet, do you know who the real heroes are? The selfless group of virtuous late-night talk show hosts (with one notable exception: me).

I don't mean the great, talented late-night hosts of the past, but the current witless activist ones of today who are all coming together to fight climate change for just one precious night. It's a perfect example of the pliable lockstep—when they all came together for "Climate Night" in September 2021 to tell us how super urgent this threat really was. It was so urgent, they had to wait until these hosts had enjoyed their entire summers off at beachfront compounds before they did it! Yeah, the planet is melting, but I'll get on it after my game of cornhole with Alec Baldwin. Which could prove fatal.

So we've gone from Carson's Carnac and Letterman's glorious stupid pet tricks to these sad sacks of panderers discussing beach erosion happening in front of their secluded seaside estates (say that three times fast and you win a back rub). Obviously, I wasn't asked to participate in this world-saving event. It's okay. I understand they don't want the profession's top talent to outshine everyone and make them all look bad.

Besides, I already had plans. Paying my bills, ironing my socks, and entertaining America.

You want to hear something hilarious? When asked why he was participating in Climate Week, Kimmel stated, "I don't want to die."

Despite doing it every night during his opening monologue. (Sorry, too easy.)

But he doesn't want to die. From what, exactly? Choking on your own tears? Colbert noted it should be more than one night, but he's too busy lecturing us on hate and other topics. And maybe taking salsa lessons with Chuck Schumer at the Arthur Murray School of Dance in Brooklyn.

I mean, if he really cared, why would he be dancing while kids are dying?

By the way, I don't want to die, either. Which is far more likely to happen on the A train, thank you.

Meanwhile, what is America really concerned about, according to poll data? Crime, homelessness, untreated mental illness, and drug addiction. Granted, those may not be typical (I think they can be) topics for comedy, but neither is this virtue-signaling climate bullshit.

But I guarantee you—I can make *all* of that funny. They can't. Because they've sold their souls to the humorlessness of wokeism.

Also, those kitchen table topics are just too hard to talk about. They require common sense, mixed with dark humor. You end up sounding like your parents, God forbid!

But climate is really easy! You can be so concerned without really sounding like an old fart. And the so-called consequences are so long term, it guarantees that none of the people pushing this shit will be held accountable later. It's like worrying about an expanding universe or the San Andreas Fault. But even more, when you're that wealthy and powerful, you can create a life that allows you to shoulder the burdens you happily impose on others. Truck drivers and plumbers are screwed when you ban gas-powered trucks, but you'll be fine in your Tesla, which you rarely drive anyway. (Also the unspoken truth: Electric cars aren't purchased as replacements, but as side pieces for gas-guzzling cars. The electric car isn't the one you choose for the road trip.)

I tell you, there's nothing funny about a hive mind that's gone full Greta Thunberg under the guise of comedy.

Meanwhile, CBS just had to cancel their new show called *The Activist* before it even aired. Activists would have competed to promote various causes, one of them being climate change. That, actually, might have been genuinely funny. Unintentionally.

But what's that really sound like? Yeah. Late-night talk show hosts, after all. Are they also competing in desperate virtue signaling so the wokeaholics don't come after them? The sad thing is, it doesn't work. CBS pulled this show because, you guessed it, it wasn't woke enough. Yep, CBS tried to go woke and the online roasters stuck their collective finger right in the CBS eye. That's the lesson. This isn't about helping people at all, but protecting your careers from the idle woke, waiting in the wings to pounce. The show was created not as entertainment but a force field for the network to protect against very lonely people whose method of achievement can only be measured in denying yours. The networks were cynical enough to play into it, and dumb enough to think it would work. I'm glad they got screwed. The Left always eat their own, eventually. Which might actually explain the new norm of fat people on magazine covers.

The Oscars might have been the most visual intersection of the terrified celebrity and sanctimonious rage. Remember how the room greeted Will Smith moments after he won for Best Actor *after* slapping Chris Rock with no immediate repercussions? That's the kind of hero's welcome reserved for me entering the steam room at Planet Fitness. But do you think these people really deserve an apology? That's one thing Jim Carrey has said in his entire life that I agree with—calling the crowd "spineless en masse." He added, "This is a really clear indication that we're not the cool club anymore."

Bull's-eye!

And why? Because they froze. The people who pretend to be "activists" about all the right causes . . . froze in a moment when real action was necessary. It was a perfect metaphor, in a way. A slap that embodied mask mandates and eighty-seven thousand new IRS agents. It was brute force, lionized.

Smith was seen dancing at an Oscar party, clutching his award like it was his bald wife. He didn't seem too traumatized, and neither did his arrogant offspring who talked trash on social media. Life went on, until it didn't.

It wasn't until the next day when they woke up and saw that the woke had deserted him. Who's laughing now? The only thing worse than Will Smith is the Oscars in general, which deserved more than a slap in the face. As they desperately tried to please the woke with their new criteria for Oscars (in which to qualify you actually have to check the sexuality of your crew members), they forgot the audience, and their own real, non-virtue-signaling morality. Maybe that morality is gone. It went out the door with their sense of humor and their balls.

It's a pretty interesting flip that Jim Carrey, to his credit, saw: the cool kids just get smaller and lamer. Next year they should all be sitting in booster seats. They went from the cheerleaders and football players at the cool table to the puniest of cowards, who sold freedom of thought and action for a sanctimonious straitjacket. And it was made clear that to make it in that industry, you had to do the same. They are the school bully who finally got what was coming to him.

I talked at length to a pretty famous comedian the other

day, who explained that in the comedy world there are two types of comics: those who have an eye on their audience and those who have an eye on Hollywood. You know the ones who love their audience (Chappelle, Louis C.K., Di Paolo, etc.) and the ones who hope they'll land a sitcom, so they play it super-safe.

It's a weird flip, to see that the edgy performer now is no different than a frightened high schooler dependent on fitting in rather than standing out. Maybe they were always that way, and it's become super obvious as they desperately seek a safe haven in an increasingly irrelevant but skittish industry.

Meanwhile, true to the flip, the ticket buyer emerges on top, offering a collective thumbs-down to the shitty woke-infested content Hollywood keeps serving up to people who prefer to get their sermons at church. It's a joy to watch cowardly virtue signaling disguised as heroic diversity fall flat on its face.

Maybe Hollywood will wake up and start making fun stuff again. But in reality, do we really give a shit? No. We're done with movies. In a few years, we won't even need the actors— they'll be done by CGI and AI. Then where on earth will all that sanctimony go? Somewhere in Silicon Valley, I suppose.

As for cable news, I'm reading Axios research that shows all cable viewership is down in prime time in the first half of the year, except, of course, for Fox News, which is up a whopping

12 percent. Axios, oddly, lumped us in with an overall decline among other networks, perhaps to hide our success.

But it's like lumping Michael Jordan in with the French army. Logically, none of this makes sense.

But one thing does: they suck and we don't. And there's a reason why.

Diversification. If you're only about one thing—Trump evil!—what happens when that tool no longer works for you? You have no more in your bag. That's why CNN nearly destroyed itself, before desperately attempting to steer itself back to some moderate degree of sanity. When a one-trick pony loses its one trick, it fears the glue factory.

But this decline is due not to news exhaustion, but to hoax exhaustion. The media and the public have flipped. It's no longer the media telling us what's news, but the reverse. The public no longer buys what the media is selling, understanding that most news is manufactured and curated for clicks and profits. Now that they know that, they dictate the terms.

It's the best flip ever.

The Losers in the Flip

I could have been a loser. (God knows I was trained for it. I mean, I did go to Berkeley.) I was pretty close, actually. In 2016, when Trump won, I was drowning in a potent mix of cognitive bias (my narrow tunnel of belief: all the world's problems are from Trump) and emotionalism (no one's listening to me that all the world's problems are from Trump). I now know who that person was—me—but I can look back and see that I was using a faulty filter.

I had ignored my friends and relatives who were gently trying to pull me back from this bottomless abyss—an abyss that swallowed up everyone from Bill Kristol to Liz Cheney, and then spit them back up as strange bitter Twitter creations, operating on the fuel of strange new respect from people who used to call them evil but now were using them to batter shared enemies.

It's sad but hilarious that Liz Cheney is accepting accolades from people who called her and her father a Nazi just years ago; now, instead of ignoring them, she embraces their style of demonization toward the very people who had given Cheney protection and a career: Republicans. That's because like her dad's heart, her moral compass is faulty. Now she calls them Nazis, just like her new friends did to her family. Instead of expressing gratitude to those who positioned her in a top-tier role of the party, she turned on them—using the same weapons that had been used against her by her new so-called friends. I've never met the lady, but I see her as a clueless bore. And those are her best qualities.

So the equation goes like this: Leftists called Liz and Dick Nazis. Then Liz calls Trump a Nazi. Now the one side who thought she was a Nazi has moved on from her because she switched sides to call Trump a Nazi. And the others she called Nazis (and also Confederate soldiers, with her being a reincarnated Abe Lincoln, with less brain matter) have told her to go fuck herself from now to forever. You got that? Me, neither. But that's okay. Because neither does Liz. Which she will discover soon enough.

How I Flipped the Conservative Script: From Dean Wormer to Animal House

In February 2022, legendary writer and humorist P. J. O'Rourke passed away at the age of seventy-four.

Saying he passed away seems very passive for someone like PJ.

People like your aunt Gladys pass away, but PJ—he just explodes and disappears.

And leaves a trail of broken bottles, smoked cigars, and sobbing women.

And annoying, obnoxious people like me, trying to emulate him. Or describe him.

When he died, I was trying to pretend it was just another

thing. Because frankly, it's not like we were super pals. And people were dying all around me. I'd lost relatives, in-laws, and friends, during Covid—from the disease, to illness exacerbated by the disease, and drug overdoses.

PJ died in the middle of all that. So it was less a shock than it was another misfortune piled on a mountain of others.

I met him when he was still very much my idol, back in the 1980s when I was a moody nobody and he was a super huge writer.

I met him again at a wedding party in the nineties. (We danced a couple times but nothing came of it.) But then thirty years later, when I got to be a huge TV star with adoring fans, a bulging bank account, and a swollen liver, I would have him on my show, and it was awesome. Like getting your favorite band to open for you, now that you're the star.

It was a generational flip. I went from peon to star. And PJ went from star to legend.

But obviously I was wrong, for many reasons.

The story hadn't flipped. I was only here because he got me here.

If anything, I was just the beginning of the next chapter, in a book begun mainly by PJ himself. And he was still kicking ass, as a thinker and editorial tinkerer.

When I met PJ for the first at the strangely unkempt *Ameri-*

can Spectator's offices, I was just an assistant, and he had shown up to see the important people (editor in chief R. Emmett Tyrell Jr., managing editor Wlady Plesczynski, and the guy I bought cigarettes for, Andy Ferguson).

I was the young kid with a buzz cut who got to tag along as we walked over to the Keyhole Tavern, a few blocks away. The Keyhole was a textbook dive, the waitstaff made up of hardened waitresses who could be anywhere from age twenty-five to forty-five, but really it was impossible to tell. They, too, were strangely unkempt. Strangely unkempt was in that year.

One thing was certain: they were women. Back then, you need not worry about having to check under the hood. They were just tough chicks. These days if you don't look under the hood you might find you're driving stick later in the evening.

They'd have one or two really cute girls, completely oblivious that they could work at a better joint. But that's the charm of being young—not knowing this. If I had known where I would be now, I never would have been doing those donkey shows in Tijuana in my twenties. That's the last time I take advice from Mike Huckabee.

The Keyhole was known for its ground beef chili over white rice—at least I hope that was rice. Every once in a while you'd catch a grain or two wiggling, but you were so fucked-up you didn't fret . . . plus it was cheap. You couldn't sit outside on their old picnic benches without getting a splinter the size of a spear in your forearm.

I'm exaggerating, but that's what you do when you can barely remember the facts. (Did I tell you about taking CornPop to the prom?)

I tagged along because I was a fanboy, at maybe twenty-one. I had devoured PJ's early books, stealing the free ones from the stack of books in the mailroom. I could quote him at length, though it's probably good that I didn't. But when he arrived, and we went to the dive, I could barely get a word out of my mouth.

I was starstruck. And in this case, PJ defied that golden rule: "never meet your heroes." I have since met a lot of my so-called heroes, and he was the most gracious of all of them.

He turned out to be as wise as I assumed, but he was also modest and gentle. I force myself to think about that now, whenever I'm in a similar situation, among younger people looking for their own path in the world. I realize that even if they can't really articulate what they want to say to me, it's not much different from me sitting with PJ at that bar. When some kid says something clumsy, I embrace it. And when some other kid tries to impress me (usually with a joke about my height—

the least original thing anyone could ever say), I give them shit.

I had read PJ's amazing magazine, *National Lampoon*, through high school, which he had edited brilliantly. It was the funniest, sharpest magazine under his watch, and his fingerprints were everywhere. He was in the photo funnies (a paneled comic that had him engaging with people, usually topless women) and his editorial letter went on forever . . . and underneath all of it was a manic sense of order. The shit made sense. He took humor very seriously. You can't be a renegade without a system; chaos is not a method to success. Underneath the fun, he put in the work.

Today I think about that, as the woke have now made their utterly insane humorlessness absolutely hysterical. The flip happened as I foresaw it when I wrote about the Dean Wormer effect maybe twenty years ago (I will get to that in a bit).

But he was the guy who showed you that you don't have to accept the way everyone else labels you. In fact, in all likelihood they're simply unimaginative and boring.

Later, after he left the *Lampoon*, PJ's essays started showing up in the *American Spectator*—an odd progression from this straight bawdy comedy. At first it was sort of like the witty class clown you knew years ago showing up at your house to sell you insurance. But *Amspec* had a similar sensibility to what one might find in *Lampoon*. It was funny and fearless, despite at times being bogged down by lengthy book reviews I could barely comprehend because my brain was still mush. Today it is fully formed mush, marinating in mushrooms and wine.

But then I started reading *Amspec* and realized it was the bridge from the *Lampoon* to what I would be doing later in life, when for fun I chose to be a writer for, of all places, the Huffington Post, when it launched.

The Huffington Post was created by, of course, Arianna Huffington, a kind of erudite redhead who if you closed your eyes sounded just like one of the Gabor sisters. But really, it was launched by some unknown crazy bastard named Andrew Breitbart. I had been asked to contribute, and that I did. But nearly all my entries targeted the elitist idiots who wrote alongside me. All along the way, Breitbart egged me on to show how absurd I viewed the enterprise. My first entry on the blog, the day it launched, was a recipe for lemon squares. Worse. In the space for my bio, if you clicked on it you'd find a secret blog shitting on everything in the universe supplying this very space to shit on them.

But as a lowly assistant in the late 1980s, I had written absolutely nothing for *Amspec*. I was too terrified. I had to start someplace that wasn't full of great writers already—it was too intimidating. This might be why I ended up in fitness—there were not a lot of Pulitzer Prize winners writing about the best spot on your ass to inject a cycle of creatine phosphate for a month. (I came close with my legendary piece "A Sixpack in 6 Minutes"—that was my *War and Peace*.)

Before I had read PJ, I was already somewhat of a right-leaning kid, but that had been a recent flip from a very superficial brand of leftism. I was a pretty strident liberal for most of my adolescence and teenage upbringing. You know, not coincidentally, when you're at your dumbest.

I was a leftist, mostly because it was romantic and naïve, and got a lot of attention from teachers and girls. It was shocking to everyone in homeroom to state that "there is no god" or "war is fascism," plus I didn't have to know really anything about that stuff to spout it. You know, like Dems talking about the economy or Republicans talking about hip-hop. It was the skeleton key to open every cool or culturally edgy door, because people found it admirable coming from a teenager, even though they were simply approving of teenage thoughts masquerading as risk—full of nothing but virtue signaling, just "look at me" bullshit. Tell teenagers this will get you attention, and they will do it even if, over time, this practice fails. I did it all the time. I'm sure if I were fifteen right now, I would be a nonbinary woodland nymph. I was an imposter—but at least I figured it out early in life. That might be my advice for anyone currently in their twenties working at places that audit TV shows or other things people actually create. . . . Get out and be your own person.

Smart people started to shake me out of my lazy assumptions and so I found myself admitting I was mostly full of shit as a liberal. It wasn't that being a liberal was de facto full of shit . . . I was just a full-of-shit liberal. I had not done the homework. I realized I didn't believe it. I was not a bleeding heart, but I could fake it. And I realized if I was doing that, and no one knew the difference, how many other libs were doing the same thing? Answer: all of Hollywood.

In high school, I found myself cruising on my liberalism, in debates and term papers. But I knew nothing. When it got exposed by fellow classmates who were smarter than me, say in debates, I would always fight back by using the same liberal ridicule (calling them warmongers, or puritans). I would always win, even though I knew I was an absolute phony.

I can't remember who suggested *Republican Party Reptile*, PJ's first political book, to me, but he opened my eyes to new possibilities. I didn't have to pretend to be something I was not. I could embrace the Right, and still be a hedonistic leftist. He showed me that the Right didn't have to look like the Right (even though he did with his khakis, blue blazer, and tie—his wardrobe made Tucker Carlson's look like Elton John's, and

Tucker showers in khakis). He swore. He partied. He wrote viciously funny shit. And he showed that the Left shouldn't own all of pop culture. Except, for now, they did.

But over time, I was going to change that. And I did.

The idea that one could be a conservative without "acting" conservative was me all over, although I hadn't known it at the time. I had spiky hair and wore leather jackets adorned with Clash, Cramps, and Sex Pistol buttons, but the people around me weren't also reading *National Review* and books by Helmut Shoeck and Whittaker Chambers.

Me before I ditched the corduroy for the Clash.

PJ's persona suggested that you could be a whole bunch of conflicting things.

Most of all, you could be fun and have fun—as much, if not more, than the leftists who pretended they were cooler. Their life was pretending they were something they were not, whether it be compassionate, empathetic, morally above it all—all pretend. That's why they get along with Hollywood celebs so well. They both act for a living.

The first time I met PJ it was awkward because I put too much emphasis on his place in my life, which is what fans do with the people they fan over.

It's something to remember when you meet your heroes: they just want you to be normal, because it keeps them normal. If they expect fandom, they're jerk faces.

So, we walked to that dismal but somehow inviting bar over the road and across the street. I was very nervous. I believe he was used to this sort of thing—people ascribe mystical talents to people they adore, and the only thing you can do is not be an idiot, and hope that they think you're not an obsessed psychopath.

A few years later, I went to see him speak, and there were dozens of young men roughly my age, dressed *exactly* like O'Rourke. Blue blazers and khakis . . . it was like Brooks Brothers started a cult, but without the group sex (thank God).

I wanted to approach him and reintroduce myself and shake

his hand, and maybe share a drink or two, but as I walked over, the Brooks brigade tensed up and closed the circle as if they were protecting a baby fawn, so I bagged it. It was the preppiest posse this side of Tucker's bachelor party.

Back when we were at the Keyhole, he made a joke about the dive being a place for knife fights. I saw my opening, and quickly said that at the Keyhole, you get thrown out if you *don't* have a knife fight. Looking back on it, I should have said the place had a two-knife minimum.

He chuckled. And it was not out of politeness' sake! It felt real.

I still kinda remember it today. Sort of word for word.

But after that I never really said a damn thing.

It's a wise thing. The less said, really, is the better. Let them talk. So instead, I drank cheap beer and listened—like most of my dates did back then.

I do remember thinking and hoping that maybe in twenty years, that would be me.

I did get to that place in life, but in a trajectory that looking back seems so bizarre.

Obviously I was inspired by PJ steering me to become what I am now . . . in that you could be anarchic, libertine, and libertarian, vote to cut taxes but do drugs—and still be a Republican. But I didn't wear khakis or blazers unless I had to. PJ made it so the Republican Party would in time welcome people like me who looked like they belonged on the other side. He made the party inviting to rebels who felt the current rebellion was clichéd and, well, conformist. This is how the Big Flip started.

How to Retrofit Your Past to Fit Your Future. Fretful About Your Future Means You're on Your Way

How does one go from being fitness editor of *Prevention* magazine to the king of late-night television?

How does that even make sense? For the people who worked with me at *Prevention*, I'm sure it can't. They saw Greg G. as the guy at the company gym who waited outside for the place to open at 5:45 a.m. They saw me as the guy who wrote, worked out three hours a day but could drink anyone under the table, and then got up the very next day and hit "repeat."

Point is, I never thought I would get to O'Rourke's stature as a writer, because understandably I had no clue and it didn't look like that's where I was headed.

National Lampoon was the opposite of something like *Prevention*. *Prevention* told you how to shave four cholesterol points off your lipid profile; *National Lampoon* taught you how to add three hundred, preferably while getting a hand job from Lynette "Squeaky" Fromme and eating a cheese steak.

But none of us have any clue what we are at that age. The fact is, I was unsure all the way up to my midthirties.

If you're reading this book, in your twenties and still unsure—that's awesome. It makes you normal.

Don't think for a second you're screwed up for not knowing where you're going. You're not failing, you're just figuring it out—and it takes longer than you want it to. You want it overnight, and it keeps you up at night. But if you work your ass off, you'll get there. Trust me. Because I did, and I did it taking more bizarre routes than a shitfaced Magellan.

I can safely say that there will never be another fitness editor who becomes the king of late night. I'm pretty sure I broke that mold. Unless Richard Simmons takes over for Trevor Noah. I hear his people have been in touch.

I did not get my first TV show until I was in my forties. Think about that. At twenty-one, that seems so far away, but it's not. A decade can fly by in an instant, especially when you're working. It takes forever when you aren't. And it will remain, *forever*, if you don't.

So what did Johnny Carson do before *The Tonight Show*? Probably split a fifth of gin with Ed McMahon and smoked half a joint with Doc Severinsen. But I mean, career-wise, what did he do?

I have no idea.

But I remember him having whitish hair when he started.

So I'm in good company.

The Flip Begins

Writing this book has forced me to rethink the impact that PJ, as well as others, has had on me, in all earnestness, because suddenly it was now the Right who were funny and the Left who weren't.

When you're looking at this flip, it goes back to PJ. It's his creation. He told people like me that you can still be a righty, but also traffic in wrongness: to be funny, loose, disgusting, horny, odd.

These were all the things that liberals could be, but we weren't allowed to be. We had created these constraints. But he showed you that you didn't always have to be puritanical, stiff, judgmental, restrained. The culture was just as much yours as I was to the Left.

The Left, they had their Abbie Hoffmans—and it was time for us to have our own, too.

It took time, but that vision is now realized.

How did that happen?

Well, my theory originally was not simply about picking a political side, but about getting politics out of your lives. The problem with this is that the other side injects politics into everything. You try to keep it amicable, but they go to the best divorce lawyer in town. So you needed to understand what they were doing, so you could turn it upside down, like Tom Brady does this to his opponent's defense. (I use this reference only to point out that Brady and I went to the same high school and since he quit, I am officially now the most successful person to come from Serra High.)

If you remember (it's okay if you don't), when I was much younger I wrote a piece called "The Dean Wormer Effect," based on the infamous dean from the 1978 movie *Animal House*.

You recall the guy—and if you don't, then put the book down and please rent *Animal House* right now, and then continue reading. You can thank or message me later.

This is what I wrote in my monologue, based on a piece I wrote in the Huffington Post about fifteen years ago. Basically I write and rewrite this idea every three or four years, to remind people that it's coming (and also I'm always repeating myself). It's like the cicada of cultural memes. The flip is coming. So here's an excerpt from that last time:

"In every situation, in real life or the media—the framework was always the same . . . we Republicans were Dean Wormer.

And the Dems were *Animal House*.

In short—we had the stick up our ass; they had a joint in their mouths."

My goal was to flip that script, to reverse the Dean Wormer effect—that to fight politics, the weapon was fun.

But now it's happening—the big flip.

We're having fun. And they are not. Especially after the 2020 election.

And we really didn't have to lift a finger.

All it took was Donald Trump, and wokeism.

Donald Trump showed us that we could be as obnoxious, feisty, and raw as them, and win.

He created millions of new nonliberals who knew how to have a good time. Trump was *fun*. The other side, not so much.

In an instant, we found ourselves laughing at the hapless CNN, which became in an instant a gibbering Dean Wormer.

In fact their entire lineup became a string of minor Wormers shaking their rakes at the clouds, tut-tutting their way to irrelevance.

Now the woke infection has turned a once-tolerant Democratic Party into one that demands psychotic adherence to an absurd regressive, angry ideology—or else you shall be banished.

The party that once said "Keep the government out of my bedroom" is now the party that says "I'll have a threesome but only if Uncle Sam is one of the three." The party that said "Sex is none of your business" is now about making gender everyone's business, and making up more of them every week.

Now they're determined to make your personal life adhere to their virtue-signaling demands.

It sounds like the Republicans we imagined from the 1950s (or even worse, the Pilgrims from the 1650s), only these are real.

Wokeism pollutes every brand it invades, because it's a political construct that forces humans to conform to unnatural demands. It puts identity above cooperation and competence.

It's an infection that "performs" its way into a party through threats of cancellation.

Once it gets in, it eats everything from the inside, like the fledgling xenomorph in *Alien*, but with less sex appeal.

Like any form of totalitarianism, they want you to fear them, to conclude that it is better to acquiesce than to combat their oppressive hysterics. Because if you say no to them, they will ruin you Even though their's is only a *performance*—as fake as a drag queen's tits.

Thanks to a pre-Elon, woke-driven Twitter, they galvanized mobs to do that very thing.

With that they turned the Democrats into the demon from *The Exorcist*—whose head spins around 360 degrees, except here it's looking for people who don't agree with them so it can vomit out pronouns, public condemnations, and moral platitudes that they can't even obey.

Now it needs an exorcism. Or at least an enema.

In my head, the exorcism is happening.

The Funny Flip

Silence tells you a lot about life. When people come after you, and then stop coming after you, what does that mean?

Why is it that the press might ignore my show as it trounces everyone else in late-night comedy? We're left off of every recap, and we get it. It's humiliating to them to see the supposedly unfunny right destroying the hilarious left-winger on their very own turf, which they once called comedy. Now they're as funny as venereal warts. Luckily, however, they're becoming easier to eradicate.

But I get the deliberate avoidance of this massive flip in the entertainment industry. It's like when your car is making a strange noise, so you turn up the radio and suddenly the noise is gone. It's like covering your eyes and sticking your fingers in your ears and singing "La la la la la." (Which is how doctors say is the safest way to get through *Fox & Friends*.) With few exceptions, the mainstream press has bent over backward to ignore our success, since ignoring it means we don't exist. There could be no viable alternative to their creed fests. True. If their minds were any more closed, they'd be a post office on the Fourth of July.

So there could be reasons for this behavior. Maybe they know they can't stand up to the challenge from this fifty-eight-year-old upstart. Their egos are too fragile. The same thing happened when Fox News launched twenty-five years ago. They laughed and mocked it—until they got stomped like bugs under a plus-size model's Crocs.

There are other signs of success that could only happen to a show that comes from the right. This information comes courtesy of Adam Carolla, whose podcast I did back in July 2022. He told me of a conversation he had with his producer who said that my show's success is arguably the biggest story in entertainment, but absolutely no one is talking about it. It's never brought up. It's the story that shall not be named.

I wasn't taking notes, but Carolla theorized that the success is such a personal affront to them that it actually hurts to talk about. It is almost like not bringing up the name of the person who betrayed you in a romantic relationship (shout-out to Taylor Swift).

When he said that, it struck me that I had scientific proof of that! I was living in an actual study where I could compare and contrast two kinds of success—that of *The Five* and that of *Gutfeld!* In the entertainment world, people could talk about *The Five*'s huge success because it wasn't their wheelhouse. To them it's what "other people" did, so the show's ripping ratings weren't a pathetic reflection on their own lack of success.

For example, the success of K-pop has no bearing on me, but if there were a five-foot-five, absolutely sexy conservative talk show host kicking my ass at night, it would be really, really hard for me to take.

So people in Hollywood can reference *The Five*. They can watch it and ridicule it, and Fox. Call us crazy or stupid or whatever—but at least they can manage to talk about it.

And I'm on that show. Yet my other show, *Gutfeld!*—they don't even criticize it. They did at the start, assuming it would fail. But its massive success has been such a direct strike into their own turf, behind enemy lines, that they can't even bring themselves to say "that shit's not funny, man" anymore. They have to pretend it doesn't exist. I think that's called being in denial. It's like the border crisis, which the Left just ignores. That sort of makes me an Ecuadoran, invading the United States of Liberalism.

And so in Hollywood, everyone does themselves the favor of never talking about me. I'm the Voldemort of late night (an Ecuadorian one).

And why? Because I flipped the script.

Just a few years ago, they were the cool kids, and Fox was the humorless scold.

Little did they know that Fox was always out for a good time, and we were on our way to having a better time. Meanwhile, they got lazy and—worse—self-serious. Since they had no competition, they realized they didn't always have to be funny or interesting or even original. They could all feed from the same political trough of assumptions—knowing that the public had nowhere else to go eat. Clapter ruled their world.

But then in their world of generic bland food, a new fresh restaurant opens up, and it's kicking all their asses. This restaurant has better food, better service, and worse—they're having a blast. They enjoy the hell out of themselves. The waitstaff isn't made up of a bunch of sullen-faced, struggling actors, doing this as a means to an end until they make it big themselves. They are actual professional waiters and waitresses who love what they do and it shows in their attitude and their work.

Meanwhile, the competition sits in silence, telling their therapists that everything is fine.

Carolla also shared a frustration with me that I had already experienced personally.

The blacklisting. It still happens. Yep, an industry that pumps out movies decrying McCarthyism every other year still happily practices it.

"It's really hard to find comedy writers for a conservative show," Carolla says, "because they know if they might work for you, or work for me—these writers won't get a gig anywhere else." It's why our show comics Joe Machi, Jamie Lissow, and Joe Devvito are so much braver than their meek peers.

It's yet another flip.

The people who claim to be anti-McCarthyism are now becoming experts at it.

I could tell you the number of actors, comedians, singers, and writers who absolutely love my show but are forbidden to do it by their agents and publicists—but this book is only a couple hundred pages long, and it would bore you to tears. I mean, who wants to hear about me running into Robert De Niro on the sidewalk and ending up wrestling him to the ground and choking him out because he wouldn't give me his agent's number, or me bitch-slapping Kevin Bacon inside a Dunkin' Donuts, right?

Sure, they can get drunk with me, but they can't do my show—ever.

They can email me and send me drunk texts—and even promise they'll come on—but if I even slightly or gently tug at them, they go radio silent.

So I don't.

But the audience doesn't miss what the audience doesn't have.

We can do just fine—and even better, I think, without A-listers.

I'll tell you why.

They can't talk about real life.

They cannot express their opinions.

In fact, some have probably never done so in their lives.

This is why when some in their late thirties decide to "get political" they come off as absolutely infantile. Paging Amy Schumer, Sarah Silverman, Leonardo DiCaprio, Brie Larson, etc.

This is what happens when you delay your intellectual growth in exchange for chasing stardom.

The perfect example is my ex, Taylor Swift. (She'll deny it, but it's okay.) I understand she's still traumatized by our breakup, and all because she refused to wear a CPAP mask to curb her snoring. She is without question an amazing talent, and a great songwriter. She spent most of her life honing her craft, and now she's probably the best at what she does.

Suddenly she discovers—wow—there's a whole world out there, and like there's really important stuff going on and jeez I can get all this strange, new respect if I align myself with stuff I barely know about. Which is also when the work begins to suffer. How long before we get "The Ballad of Roe v. Wade" or "Solar Power Rhapsody" from her?

Celebrity activism is often born from a desire to shed the appearance of shallowness for depth. Look, I'm not just a pretty girl singer—I have deep thoughts! Here, listen to this one: "It's getting warmer outside! We need to cool the planet!"

But at least Swift is acting on her beliefs. I just read she sold one of her two private jets. She really hated the color scheme, and I don't blame her. I scrapped one of my helicopters because the radio couldn't get in my favorite Spanish soaps.

So as the show continues to flip the late-night landscape, we start hearing of changes.

CNN is moving away from their activist leftism. They might even return to news! CBS is going to do a late-night comedy panel; so is Comedy Central (didn't they do this before?). As I write this, Colbert and Fallon are taking pot shots at Biden (granted they're risk-free, benign jokes). Suddenly people are finding out that yes, you can make fun of Democrats! I know, it's like discovering the Dead Sea Scrolls. This is a direct result of this show, *Gutfeld!*

Of course, Bill Maher has made a transition that would make Caitlyn Jenner blush. To be fair, his show has never been better. He still skewers the Right (as he should), but now he's equally vicious if not more to the loons on the left.

Other comedians are not afraid to leave the liberal reservation. Russell Brand. Joe Rogan. Dave Chappelle. Bill Burr. However, I want you to note that even though a few of these guys waited until they had made their coin first before making the jump, as opposed to let's say Nick Di Paolo, a brilliant comedian who you've probably never heard of because he didn't wait until he was rich or famous before he flipped Hollywood the bird, thus stunting his showbiz career but gaining the respect of his comedian peers, which he'll be the first to tell you doesn't exactly up his price when doing a live venue. But he says he sleeps well at night, often alone but well. (Note: I added this in because Nick wrote that graph and has a picture of me naked straddling Burgess Meredith.)

True, there are still a sad bunch of "alternative" comics who cling to their woke blankets, hating on all the others. But to call them comics now, well, it's not really fair.

I'm saying that as a noncomedian.

But someone had to go there first. To go "full right" late at night.

I'm not saying I'm the one. I'm just the one to do it at late night and throw it in their faces. There will be more, and hopefully even better ones.

Now they're seeing that it's okay to have a diversity of opinion.

It's okay to make fun of people that you might actually see at your next cocktail party. It's okay to speak your mind—in fact others really need to hear it, because they have those thoughts too.

But maybe I'm wrong.

I maintain that I am not a comedian at all.

I have never done stand-up, because that late at night in a club, I can't stand up anyway.

I was an editor in chief.

I wrote and edited for a living. I never went out "on the road," except for my Kerouac period, which I will be recounting in a forthcoming six-volume set of poetry.

I never stayed in cheap hotels and picked up bored waitresses. (Well, not as a comedian—but when I was dancing for Chippendales . . . that's another story.)

And when I do my live shows for my book tour, I actually sit most of the time, onstage, and do a slide show. That's not really a comedian act.

So if I were to say I'm a comedian, I would consider that "stolen valor."

But Carolla told me that I was lying to myself. Those things—the chair, the slide show, calling it a book tour—these are all crutches that you don't need.

It's time to flip from noncomic to comic—because in the end, it will make you better, and you'll like it even more.

So maybe that's next.

THE AFTER PARTY

And How to Join It

I have no interest in being a Republican, a Democrat, or a Libertarian.

Don't even mention the Green Party. Anyone who worships the almighty dollar makes me sick.

Parties suck.

I was always more of a fan of the "after parties."

You know: the thing, after the thing. When the people at the first thing already are in an Uber heading to a Marriott Express for a sound sleep.

As a men's magazine editor in my thirties, I threw more than a few of them, and they were always more fun than that initial party celebrating a new movie, or the debut of whatever

new vacuous cover girl who would end up marrying Dennis
Rodman. And then divorcing Dennis Rodman. And then
remarrying Dennis Rodman.

Those parties were usually reserved for promoters, ad salesmen, and unsightly staffers. Generally they lasted two hours,
consisted of sweaty people doing lines of badly stepped-on
cocaine in bathrooms, morose security on walkie-talkies trying to ignore the impatient sniffers, and throngs of glassy-eyed
bros eyeing the only two models present—Eastern European
types desperately waiting for a Wilson brother to show up to
bang in a closet (usually it was Owen). They were banal, conformist affairs. I would skip them and always head to the after
party.

Which often, happily, was no party at all.

It was just for the interesting, quiet people who kept to
themselves in a dark bar, or someone's house in the hills. People
were kind, no roughhousing, and the drugs were way better.

You see where I am going with this.

It's time for the After Party.

The next thing after the Republican, Democrat, and Libertarian parties.

Those parties are dead. And they can't revive themselves.

What's the After Party, you ask?

It's the party for people like you and me who aren't slaves

to ideologies, who aren't slaves to the prison of two ideas, the duopoly. In fact, we may be entirely nonideological. We may disagree on everything, but then be hardly disagreeable at all. We want to be proven wrong, rather than have our beliefs validated in a bubble. We see politics as a buffet. We can pick what we like, and not have to inhale everything.

To summarize the After Party: it is a place for red-pilled grown-ups to be honest about the world, without worrying about being ruined for it. We are outside this duopoly, and the media industrial complex. We see the world for what it is. We don't play team sport politics. We play for the bigger reward: enlightenment.

The After Party's Principles

Reject the Worst Stereotype

To quote the Scott Adams rule of jerks:

If you think a group of people can be fairly defined by the worst person in the group, the worst person in your group is you.

The goal of the After Party: to assume the best in people, not the worst.

This is important as you evolve (an elitist term for "getting older").

When I was a teen, I was a lefty, and I saw everyone on the right as evil. I defined the Right as the worst person in their group. Then when I got to college and saw real leftism up close, I switched sides and became a righty. But still: I had committed that sin—I defined the other side by the worst person in their group. I had gotten smarter, but not by much. Once I shed that reflex, I grew. Not literally grew. That was impossible by that age. But you get the idea.

Defend Those Who Are Under Attack

Has the Republican Party ever tried to save anyone from being canceled? Have they ever stuck their neck out for anyone? Nope. They only leap to your defense when it's safe. Unlike Trump. He never hesitated to defend people under attack. Did Mitt Romney ever defend anyone? Republicans only defend Republicans when there's no chance of blowback. So you owe them nothing. But Trump never piled on, when the going got rough. Hate him all you want, but he had no hesitation in absorbing your risk.

The After Party's goal is to provide a barrier against cancel culture. We don't need to defend losers but we should protect those who are considered odd. We need to reject the annihilation of people simply because they're weird. But not "looks" weird; I mean "ideas" weird. (Looking weird is easy, thinking weird is groundbreaking.) Here's why: no one else will do it.

Corporations won't do it. Comedians won't even do it for their friends. Hell, even family members won't do it. We need a real movement to counter what is currently eating this country from the inside: conformity fascists who wish to punish you for rejecting their own political performance. These are lemmings violently angry that you aren't leaping off a cliff with them. I pushed this hard in my last book, *The Plus*: if we share the risk against the mob, the mob flees back under their collective rocks.

Hire and Protect the Renegades, Messy Thinkers, and Risk-Takers

What makes this crazy orb go round are the very people being targeted by the banal members of the media-academic-industrial complex. The moment you see someone who thinks outside the box being fitted for a coffin, you'd better stand up and defend them. You know who those people are. One of them is Dave Rubin. Leaving the Left could have ruined him, but instead the sensible souls of the world welcomed and defended him, and now he is a media mogul sending me checks every week. Which actually clear (unlike the checks I get from Larry Kudlow for scrubbing the jets in his jacuzzi).

Seek Out People to Prove You Wrong, Not Right

I believe all drugs should be legal. Sold over the counter. At Walgreens. At Duane Reade.

No prescription necessary.

"Even heroin, Greg?" you ask.

"Especially heroin," I say.

Does that mean I want to sit around and discuss how great legalizing drugs would be—because I already know that to be true? No. I would rather hear cogent arguments disagreeing with me, to test the strength of my own beliefs.

I've made some mistakes in my life by ignoring people or ridiculing them, simply because they held different beliefs. And it didn't serve me well. Back in my Huffington Post days, fifteen years ago or so, I would mock people like Glenn Greenwald, Bill Maher, and Matt Taibbi, among others. I had my reasons, but I bet they weren't well tested, because I wasn't so much interested in seeing my ideas challenged. I now enjoy it. I also enjoy Greenwald, Maher, and Taibbi—and see in them stuff I obviously missed way back when. That's on me, not them.

Do Not Let Others Tell You Who You Can or Can't Talk To

The cancellers will play a game of *contact contamination*—and here's an example tied to me:

A very hip musician happens to be an acquaintance of mine, and we chat periodically about stuff, usually in Twitter DMs. One day he emailed me and said that he'd been contacted by a well-known music publication that had noticed that he followed me on Twitter (a mortal sin), and they wanted to know why.

The message was obvious: "If you follow Greg Gutfeld, we'll do a story on it, and it won't be good for you." And this time, it wasn't a collection agency.

This happens a lot, to me.

You saw what happened to Ariel Pink for showing up to a rally to support Trump on January 6. His music label dropped him, even though he was in his hotel room during the riot, showing what cowards that label was.

What's interesting to me: how you get punished for having far more interesting friends, and a far more interesting life, than the actual punishers, who are generally very unlikable, boring people who only want to be surrounded by the same.

Be a Plus, Not a Minus

It would be good if you read my book *The Plus*, but you don't have to. The After Party is a party for positive people. For people who want to engage with other people about stuff that interests them, politically and culturally. If you just say everything sucks and it's hopeless, then you miss out on your ability to affect life itself. *You can make it better.* That was the essence of *The Plus*.

The bottom line: it's really all about culture. And we need to win some of it back. Or it will be all gone soon.

So to answer your questions:

How do you join the After Party? If you read this, and you liked it: you just did.

Will the After Party present candidates for election? Maybe. That's a lot of work. But sure, why not? I would like one day to be mayor of a major city. Or even a minor one. Actually, I just want to run anything where I can ban weird stuff like mass theft and public defecation. Also, Maroon 5.

What do I hope to accomplish? A real party with real people who are willing to fight the cancel culture woke brigade to the very end. If there's nobody willing to do this, then let it be us, for fuck's sake. Which is not a bad campaign slogan actually.

Okay, so who's in charge of the After Party?

For now, it's you and me.

ACKNOWLEDGMENTS

The more books I do, the longer the acknowledgments get. Because you just end up relying on so many people, and it adds up. Frankly, I could just do a book on the acknowledgements that enable my life. (Hmmm . . . that's my next book!) But in this case, I'm gonna keep it short. Because good things come in small packages, including of course, me.

First I gotta thank Fox for this tremendous opportunity: Suzanne Scott, Rupert Murdoch, Lachlan Murdoch, and everyone who didn't need convincing to hand over five more quality hours of programming a week to a miscreant like me. I know I am good at this stuff, but I also know that I am a risk—every time I open my mouth I jump off a cliff.

All the people at Fox, from my great producers, like Tom O'Connor, who runs *Gutfeld!*, and Megan Albano, to the deeply talented staffs who work with me and have to put up with my cryptic desires for a show no one has done before. None of this would be possible without the amazing *Gutfeld!* team.

ACKNOWLEDGMENTS

I have to thank Gabrielle Penner for assisting me in this book, as well as the show, and *The Five*. Kat and Tyrus have made me look better than I deserve to look. The fabulous crew of *The Five* truly define the real meaning of tolerance when they deal with me. I admit I am no day at the beach. In fact, to paraphrase my own criticism of Trump, I'm basically two hours of driving to get one hour at the beach. But it's a good hour. Thanks to Dana Perino for making me watchable. And to Jesse Watters for making me appear smart by comparison.

Of course, I gotta thank my manager, Aric Webb, who's been with me since the days of *Stuff* magazine. Boy does he have stories, and you'll never hear those—which is why he is the greatest manager you could have. Kudos to him for landing a lovely wife, Ann. And Jay Mandel—he took a chance on me back in 2006 or so at a dinner party for Piers Morgan. Now nearly twenty years later, we continue to kick ass and take fat advances, to which I spend on wine and dog toys.

Many warm thanks to my editor, Natasha Simons, who is a pleasure to work with—so much that I will deliberately ignore that she is one of those weird adult fans of Disneyland theme parks. Everyone has kinks. Which means, I cannot cast a stone.

Of course, I gotta thank Tucker for persuading me to take a risk I was ready to decline completely. My life would be different, for sure, if I ignored his advice.

I gotta thank those who read this manuscript and gave me suggestions and jokes: Paul Mauro, Nick Di Paolo, Dolph Lungren.

I hate it when some of the best lines are theirs, so I won't tell you which ones they are.

As aways, I gotta thank my family, who helped me out when I was under stress with a new show, another book, and of course, a new dog.

Here's Gus:

Thanks to all the help from my sister, Leslie, when I was about to collapse under my canine care incompetence.

Thanks to the buddies: Buzzo, Scott, Tarlov, Emily, Joey, Shillue, Jamie L, Vincent g, Keith the gymnast, Arash, Gene, Dagen, John Rich, the great Walter Kirn (for sage wisdom), Joe Escalante, Rob Long, Mark Rozario (for great ideas), Kilmeade (for being a great foil on the show), Harold Ford (junior!), the Gale family, Dave Rubin, Dianne Brandi, Kudlow, Jerry Only, Chuck (Dusty RIP), RJ (close personal friend—thanks for the guitar lessons), Trey Yingst (for being there), and Steve Harrigan (you're the best). And if I left anyone out, it's only because I'm lazy and stupid.